QUEER POLITICS IN INDIA

Queer Politics in India simultaneously tells two interconnected stories. The first explores the struggle against violence and marginalization by queer people in the Indian subcontinent, and places this movement towards equality and inclusion in relation to queer movements across the world. The second story, about a lesbian suicide in a small village in India, interrupts the first one, and together, these two stories push and pull the book to elucidate the failure and promise of queer politics, in India and the rest of the world.

This book emerges at a critical time for queer politics and activism in India, exploring the contemporary queer subject through the different lenses of critical psychology, Lacanian psychoanalysis, feminist and queer theory, and cultural studies in its critique of the constructions of discourses of 'normal' sexuality. It also examines how power determines further segregations of 'abnormal' sexuality into legitimate and illegitimate queer subjectivities and authentic and inauthentic queer experiences. By allowing a multifaceted and engaged critique to emerge that demonstrates how the idea of a universal queer subject fails lower class, lower caste queer subjects, and queer people of colour, the author expertly highlights how all queer people are not the same, even within queer movements, as the book asks the questions, "which queer subject does queer politics fight for?", and, "what is the imagination of a queer subject in queer politics?"

This hugely important and timely work is relevant across many disciplines, and will be useful for students of psychology and other academic areas, as well as researchers and activist organizations.

Shraddha Chatterjee is currently a PhD scholar in Gender, Feminist, & Women's Studies at York University, Toronto. She has previously trained in psychology, and her work is informed by Lacanian psychoanalysis, critical psychology, feminist and queer theory, and cultural studies. She is involved with feminist queer spaces in New Delhi and Kolkata.

Concepts for Critical Psychology:
Disciplinary Boundaries Re-thought
Series editor: Ian Parker

Developments inside psychology that question the history of the discipline and the way it functions in society have led many psychologists to look outside the discipline for new ideas. This series draws on cutting edge critiques from just outside psychology in order to complement and question critical arguments emerging inside. The authors provide new perspectives on subjectivity from disciplinary debates and cultural phenomena adjacent to traditional studies of the individual.

The books in the series are useful for advanced level undergraduate and postgraduate students, researchers and lecturers in psychology and other related disciplines such as cultural studies, geography, literary theory, philosophy, psychotherapy, social work and sociology.

Most recently published titles:

Queer Politics in India
Towards Sexual Subaltern Subjects
Shraddha Chatterjee

Subjectivity, Language and the Postcolonial
Beyond Bourdieu in South Africa
Hannah Botsis

Blackwashing Homophobia
Violence and the Politics of Sexuality, Gender and Race
Melanie Judge

Self Research
The Intersection of Therapy and Research
Ian Law

The Therapeutic Turn
How Psychology Altered Western Culture
Ole Jacob Madsen

Race, Gender, and the Activism of Black Feminist Theory
Working with Audre Lorde
Suryia Nayak

QUEER POLITICS IN INDIA
Towards Sexual Subaltern Subjects

Shraddha Chatterjee

LONDON AND NEW YORK

First published 2018
by Routledge
2 Park Square, Milton Park, Abingdon, Oxon OX14 4RN

and by Routledge
711 Third Avenue, New York, NY 10017

Routledge is an imprint of the Taylor & Francis Group, an informa business

© 2018 Shraddha Chatterjee

The right of Shraddha Chatterjee to be identified as author of this work has been asserted by her in accordance with sections 77 and 78 of the Copyright, Designs and Patents Act 1988.

All rights reserved. No part of this book may be reprinted or reproduced or utilised in any form or by any electronic, mechanical, or other means, now known or hereafter invented, including photocopying and recording, or in any information storage or retrieval system, without permission in writing from the publishers.

Trademark notice: Product or corporate names may be trademarks or registered trademarks, and are used only for identification and explanation without intent to infringe.

British Library Cataloguing-in-Publication Data
A catalogue record for this book is available from the British Library

Library of Congress Cataloging-in-Publication Data
Names: Chatterjee, Shraddha, author.
Title: Queer politics in India : towards sexual subaltern subjects / Shraddha Chatterjee.
Description: Abingdon, Oxon ; New York, NY : Routledge, 2018. | Includes bibliographical references.
Identifiers: LCCN 2017060862 (print) | LCCN 2017061134 (ebook) | ISBN 9781315178509 (Ebk) | ISBN 9781351713573 (Adobe) | ISBN 9781351713566 (ePub) | ISBN 9781351713559 (Mobipocket) | ISBN 9781138036529 (hbk) | ISBN 9781138036536 (pbk)
Subjects: LCSH: Gays—India. | Feminist theory. | Queer theory.
Classification: LCC HQ76.3.I4 (ebook) | LCC HQ76.3.I4 C43 2018 (print) | DDC 306.76/60954—dc23
LC record available at https://lccn.loc.gov/2017060862

ISBN: 978-1-138-03652-9 (hbk)
ISBN: 978-1-138-03653-6 (pbk)
ISBN: 978-1-315-17850-9 (ebk)

Typeset in Bembo
by Florence Production Ltd., Stoodleigh, Devon, UK
Printed and bound by CPI Group (UK) Ltd, Croydon, CR0 4YY

To those who live and die without a trace

CONTENTS

Preface ix
Acknowledgements xi

1 Post-script 1

2 Fragmentary fields: a map of queer politics in India 11

3 Queer/political/subject 37

4 Inside the fold of re-presentations 69

5 Towards sexual subaltern subjects 93

6 Melancholy, uncertainty, responsibility 119

Bibliography 129
Index 137

PREFACE

Towards sexual subaltern subjects

It was said in the early days of queer theory that, when this radically corrosive adjectival form 'queer' has been crystallized into an identity to be claimed as part of the apparatus of citizenship, it would be time to move on. What was disturbingly progressive about queer would then be dead. This book is about death, and it is about the stakes of reaffirming the difference between individual 'good subjects' of the polity and sexual subaltern subjects who are, if it is possible to say this, authentically divided, true to what they are becoming precisely because they refuse to speak within the empirically correct categories of individual identity that the nation-state and the discipline of psychology revel in.

It is clear that there is still a good deal of resistance to the incorporation of queer into the well-worn tracks of identity, and this resistance is cleverly amplified in *Queer Politics in India* by drawing on psychoanalytic and postcolonial theory, marking out a place for the queer subject to speak and contrasting it with a psychological notion of individuality that rests on citizenship, equal rights, and inclusion. There must, of course, be a historical element to this story, of the history of particular queer subjects – here we have Swapna and Sucheta repeatedly intervening in the text – and of the history of the context in which they speak, here it is India. Here in the book we have a crafted narrative about difference and about the concepts we must develop to keep that narrative alive.

Sexual subaltern subjects are 'outwith' every form of identity, and so provide the most radical critique of psychology. And in this particular context, as sexual subaltern subjects in India, they exist outwith the West as geographical and imperial sources of a rapidly globalizing psychological knowledge and instrument of surveillance determining who can speak and what they should say about themselves. These subjects are, in this sense, living concepts that Shraddha Chatterjee traces in this outstanding book, tracing both how they operate outside the domain of acceptable discourse, operating as a critical counterpoint to what we take for granted about ourselves and about postcolonial subjects in India, and how they operate inside the margins of experience, questioning from the inside what we must be to be fully-consciously whole human beings. One of the lessons of psychoanalysis, especially queered psychoanalysis, is that there is no such thing as a fully-conscious whole human being, and so we must listen now to the voices of those who are dead but who still speak of their lives so that we might all live better, different, outwith a queer politics of difference.

Ian Parker
University of Manchester

ACKNOWLEDGEMENTS

These words have become a book because of Ian Parker, who saw in my work what I could not. My work became what it was because of the guidance, friendship, and love extended to me by Rukmini Sen, who was my supervisor when I was writing the thesis that has eventually become this book. This book is stitched together by the kindness the participants of this work have shown me, and I will carry their stories with me for a long time; these words are as much theirs as they are mine. The excerpts of interviews I provide in this book come from my fieldwork for this research, and with permission from my participants. The letter left by Swapna that intersperses this book comes from *Sappho for Equality*'s archives, given to me during my MPhil research. At Taylor and Francis, I am thankful to Eleanor Reedy and Alex Howard, for patiently and warmly handling all my questions. At Florence Production, I want to thank Richard Sanders and Charlotte Parkins for editing this work.

At the Centre for Women's Development Studies, I am grateful to Mary John for her teachings and feedback during my MPhil years. I am thankful for the engagement and comments of Asha Achuthan and Navaneetha Mokkil, who were the examiners of my thesis. I have benefited from my participation at the Cultural Studies Workshop organized by the Centre for Studies in Social Sciences, Calcutta in 2016, where conversations with Anirban Das and Kiran Keshavamurthy, and suggestions by Trina Nileena Banerjee, furthered the ideas in this book.

In Bengaluru, I have had the good fortune of knowing Sumathy Murthy and Sunil Mohan, extraordinary people with extraordinary minds, whose hospitality mattered enormously as I grappled with this thesis. In Mumbai, I am grateful to Chayanika Shah, Shals Mahajan, Smriti Nevatia, and Raj Merchant for their time, conversations, and insight. To Abhisikta, I owe the gift of truth and friendship. In Kolkata, I send my unfailing love to everyone at *Sappho for Equality*, without whom my questions would not even be syllables, because of whom I know Swapna and Sucheta. To Sutanuka and Poushali, I am thankful beyond words can say for their friendship, anger, questions, and presence. To Lipi Di, I am grateful for her hospitality and her uniqueness.

To Karuna Chandrashekar, I owe much more than friendship; her perspective teaches me patience and poetry. To Sabah Siddiqui, I owe more than I know; her support and kindness has allowed this work to occur. To the erstwhile Lacan Reading group – Hsing-Wen Chang, Wing-Kwong Wong, and Shyamolima Ghosh – I owe many learnings on Lacan and life. To Kimberly Lacroix, whose far away presence still matters, I owe a surprising lesson in strength. To Shifa Haq, I owe care that emerges from an unlikely place. To my students at Ambedkar University Delhi and York University, I owe the happiness, energy, and hopefulness that helped me write and edit this book.

This book would not have been possible without the labour of my mother, which ensured I had enough time and space to write and think. I am thankful to my grandmother and father for their care and their conversations. I inherit a love of reading from both my grandfathers, who would have been proud to see this book in its final form. To Priyanka Shokeen and Cleo, I owe my ability to breathe; they are the magic in this cruel world. Lastly, to the memory of Alex, I owe my entire life, existence, and being.

1
POST-SCRIPT

'Queer' has become a repository of many things over time. To *be* queer is an identity; to *live* a queer life is embodiment; to *do* queer things is action, doing something *queerly/queering* something are processes. For each use of the word 'queer', we can ask – what does it mean to be queer, to live a queer life, to do queer things, to do something queerly, to queer something? More importantly, perhaps, who is queer and who is not, is there a blueprint of a queer life, what is a queer thing and what is not, is there a benchmark beyond which something is queered? And perhaps the most difficult, do all queer subjects live a queer life? Who or what decides the parameters of queerness, the spectrum on which one subject is 'more queer' than another? It is somewhere amid these questions that a politics of queerness (as opposed to a *queered* politics) reveals itself, and these questions are kept open as I attempt to map queer politics and queer subjectivity in this book.

Queerness is dynamic, it changes forms and articulations upon each utterance; and yet, queerness is also stable, marked in difference to heterosexuality and, sometimes, heteronormativity (Butler, 1990; Sedgwick, 1990; Halberstam, 1998). Like the preface that pre-determines entry into a text, and a text that simultaneously upholds and annuls the preface (Spivak, 1976/2002), queerness remains fixed at the level of its signification as that which is different from heterosexuality and/or binary genders, but is flexible in how that difference is interpreted and performed in everyday life. Each utterance of queerness has the potential to reveal the limits of heterosexuality and binary genders, but it is not necessary that all acts, moments, or performances of queerness will actualize that potential. In such an understanding of queerness as embodiment/way of life/orientation/political strategy (Ahmed, 2006), where it represents an incommensurate difference from heterosexuality and conventional gender norms, there is a segregation of queer subjects as political or apolitical that, if explored, comes close to answering some of the questions asked above.

'Queer' is often also (only) about sexuality and the gender binary. It is, for the most part, defined based on who you are or are not attracted to, have sex with or do not, and hinged on where you consider yourself to be on the gender spectrum that exists between conventional masculinity and conventional femininity. This limits the possibilities of manoeuvring trans narratives beyond masculinity and femininity and restricts them to either upholding or opposing binary gender. It also reduces sexuality to the sexual act, and this stratification of sexualities reduces their field of signification and leaves other manifestations of sexuality outside its discourses. These discourses of sexuality are also largely determined by a history of sexuality that emerges in Western contexts (Foucault, 1978), and are generative of a kind of sexual subject that is located in those cultures. Here, sexuality is a domain of truth and the deployment of power, defining the knowledge of queerness, its nature, and its limits.

The politics of queerness that emerge in such contexts, which determine what will fall within the field of queer politics and outside it, and help differentiate between who comes to be seen as a queer subject and to what degree, do so by producing certain discourses of queer sexuality at the cost of erasing others. Queerness becomes an isolated identity and helps invisibilize power imbalances between queer subjects (Upadhyay & Ravecca, 2017). After all, "[i]dentity is what we bequeath, not what we inherit, what we invent, not what we remember" (Darwish, 2009, p. 156). It is not surprising that a radical critique of heterosexuality and the gender binary emerges alongside a critique of queer identity politics from spaces that are attuned to the segregations of race, colour, and class (Haritaworn, 2017). To universalize queer subjectivity is to erase narratives of queer people of colour and un-see class differences within queer subjects; it is to promote the unrealistic promise of solidarity that queer identity politics cannot deliver while refusing the possibility of racist and capitalist supremacy in such politics (Judge, 2018). The seduction of pinkwashing and the effectiveness of homonationalism demonstrate the complicity of queer politics in various parts of the world with nationalist, colonial, and neoliberal agendas (Puar, 2017).

It seems that queer politics in India, insofar as it sees queerness as insulated and restricted to sexual identity, also carries these dangers, and often actualizes violence against those subjected to its politics. Perhaps the Indian State's assimilationist strategies can already be seen in the after-effects of the Rights of Transgender Persons Bill of 2014 and the Transgender Persons (Protection of Rights) Bill of 2016, which have sparked debates within transgender communities about which subjects classify as transgender and the processes behind such classification. In India, where male-to-female transgender visibility and collectivization far outstrips any articulations by female-to-male transgender subjects, within queer spaces and outside them, these bills have further sharpened the divide between the two groups, making female-to-male transgender subjects feel even more oppressed and ostracized (Sutanuka, Shraddha, & Poushali, 2014). However, perhaps because of the State's reticence to dispense with Section 377, homonationalism has not yet actualized its potential in queer politics in India and pinkwashing remains removed from its horizons, even as its threat looms large. Strong critiques of capitalism from within queer spaces ensure that most Pride marches in India remain free from corporate funding, and an intersectional approach that links caste and queerness is germinating. Because both caste and queerness are about who we can and cannot touch, intimately, privately and publicly, their intersection provides a productive possibility of imagining queer politics as contestation and resistance.

As such, *Queer Politics is India* is all these things and more. It imagines queer politics as operating "both with and against circuits of power and politics . . . as an embodiment of both discipline and its defiance" (Judge, 2018, p. 7), as a space of complicity and critique, and positions itself at the border-zones, searching along its interstices for that which has been lost and that which can be found. In this book, I have tried to preserve a strong sense of all these contestations while narrating one story of queer politics in India among many. The next three chapters are influenced by my work with three groups that work on lesbian, bisexual, and transmen rights – *Sappho for Equality* in Kolkata, *LABIA* in Mumbai, and *LesBit* in Bengaluru, my experiences of queer spaces in New Delhi, and on dialogues that emerged in national consultations organized by *LABIA* in 2015 and *Sappho for Equality* in 2017. This is supplemented by research that emerges from and about queer politics in India (*Caleri*, 1999; Fernandez, 2002; Narrain & Bhan, 2005; Basu, 2006; *Sappho for Equality*, 2010, 2011; *LABIA*, 2013; Katyal, 2016; khanna, 2016).

Even though the book tries to capture queer politics in India, it noticeably misses articulations of queerness from Southern and Northeastern India, and does not place transgender subjects in the history of such politics. To some extent, both absences are about the necessary limits of the scope of this book, and largely based on the link between queerness and culture. Different parts of India have different articulations of queerness that rely on geographically specific cultural histories. Similarly, a larger game is at play with respect to transgender subjectivities in India that goes beyond gender or sexuality; the contemporary transgender subject in India finds itself caught between a fading voice of colonialism from the past and the strong pull of globalization in the present. Moreover, no documentation of queer politics in India can be complete; the multiplicity of queer voices and segregations between queer subjects ensure that any mapping of queer politics in India remains one among many queer scripts.

When Swapna and Sucheta Mondal were found dead on 21 February 2011, on the outskirts of Sonachura, in Nandigram, West Bengal, their death became a part of this segregated and many-tongued queer politics. They had ingested pesticide, and died embracing each other. Their bodies were not claimed by their families, and they were cremated close to Nandigram police station one week later. A fact-finding team from *Sappho for Equality* went to Sonachura on 26 February 2011, and again nine months later. From their investigations emerged a fact-finding report, a preliminary document that was circulated among other lesbian, gay, bisexual, transgender, and queer (henceforth, LGBTQ) groups and organizations across India. In 2013, Swapna's and Sucheta's deaths, and Swapna's suicide letter, became part of the documentary titled *Ebong Bewarish* (. . . *And the Unclaimed*), produced by *Sappho for Equality*.

Since their death comes to us as a lesbian suicide, claimed by queer activists to demonstrate how queer lives are continuously unclaimed, the question that formed the roots of this book was whether queer politics in India would have made space for Swapna and Sucheta had they been alive, and what the place of their subjectivities would have been in the topology of such politics. This necessitated a mapping of queer politics in India on the one hand, and an attempt to understand Swapna and Sucheta's place as queer subjects among other queer subjects affecting and affected by such politics on the other hand. This divided path moved this book in apposite directions. The circuitous routes it takes, and the disciplines it rests on and wrests from are a way to demonstrate how Swapna and Sucheta were absent from queer politics in India, even as this politics lay its claim on them after their death. This absence is not an absolute one, but one that is grounded in processes that misrepresent Swapna and Sucheta as lesbian subjects. Swapna and Sucheta's place in queer politics in India seems to be a metonymized one, where they are subjected to – but not agential subjects of – such politics.

It is the absent acknowledgement of their difference from other queer subjects who author queer politics and the forgetting of their subjectivities when imagining a queer subject that pushed the central thesis of this work *Towards Sexual Subaltern Subjects* who lie at the "limits of truth" (Derrida, 1993), insofar as truth is determined by knowledge structures that put such subjects outside their borders. The last two chapters are therefore about thinking through why Swapna and Sucheta are sexual subaltern subjects, what it may mean to be such a subject, and what it might demonstrate about queer politics in India. The sexual subaltern subject may serve as a reminder to – and remainder of – a queer politics in India that is at risk of forgetting the problems of increasingly insular and identitarian politics that is driven towards inclusive citizenship despite its psychic and political costs.

In many ways, this book is a reconstructive project, piecing together narratives, stories, and histories to produce a coarse, interdisciplinary text that tries to find sexual subaltern subjects at its interstices. My own framework with which to understand sexuality has shifted from psychiatry and mainstream psychology, to psychoanalysis, critical psychology, and feminist and queer theories in a way that tries to bring together psychoanalytic and political theorizations of subjectivity. This shift in perspectives also determines the nature of this work.

For me, psychiatry and psychology, with their history of characterizing queerness as abnormality, perversion, and deviance (Davidson, 2001; Foucault, 2003; Tosh, 2015), and psychoanalysis, standing divided on whether to celebrate the 'polymorphous perversities' that Freud (1905) theorized as intrinsic to psychoanalytic subjectivity, were not fully able to provide non-pathological frameworks with which we could understand queer sexuality. Even though psychoanalysis could demonstrate how everyday life was replete with sexual motivations, which became a fertile ground on which to build an understanding of human subjectivity

(Parker, 2011), critiques of some branches of psychoanalytic theory and practice demonstrated how they interiorized the subject by reinforcing a strong division between what is inside the subject (psyche) and what is outside the subject (society).

The task of critical psychology, then, could be seen to be two-fold – first, to make visible and critique the frameworks of psychiatry, psychology, and psychoanalysis that intend to normalize the subject in the name and norm of cure, and, second, to discover and build effective models of psychological care that can see the individual subject as not only within the boundaries of interiority and as patients who needed to be cured of pathologies that were necessarily internal, but as persons (often belonging to communities) whose symptoms were responses to society and culture. In other words, the task is to reveal the workings of power within circuits of psychiatry, psychology, and psychoanalysis, which we now know are linked to global capital and economies that sustain relations of colonization (Mills, 2014). The added challenge of critical psychology in India, with its history of colonialism, is to provide a robust model of psychotherapy and subjectivity that is emblematic of critical cultures and its resultant subjectivities (Siddiqui, 2016). It is to think through the subject as an extimate one, to shift from a model of interiority to a frame of exteriority.

This shift to critical psychology, for me, required a necessary turn to queer and feminist theories, which have historically critiqued psychiatry, psychology, and psychoanalysis as reinforcing patriarchal and heterosexual structures (Beauvoir, 1949/2011; Mitchell, 1974; Butler, 1990; Chesler, 2005), claiming that the grounds of these knowledge systems are stacked against queer subjects (Sedgwick, 1990; Rubin, 2011). These critiques, attuned to the ways in which sexuality is discursively interiorized and localized in the subject, attempt to move towards the production of a sexual self that cannot remain within the bounds of the psyche, but is influenced by society, culture, and political economy (Oliviera, Costa, & Carniero, 2014).

It is this history that is at work in the way that this research is framed, where the politics of the sexual and sexuality are not necessarily the same, and where the task is to think through hitherto given discourses of what sexuality means, and what it can mean in the future. As such, this book is also an attempt to bridge the gap between psychoanalysis and politics while remaining aware that both disciplines need to be rethought in order to be brought to a dialogue. In both psychoanalysis and political theory, there is a sustained theorization of the subject – both schools of thought are concerned with resistance and transformation. However, psychoanalytic resistance is not the same as political resistance, and both disciplines have distinct but potentially overlapping ideas of transformation. Further, as this book is about sexual subaltern subjects, it hopes to take an extra step towards placing such subjects at the centre of psychoanalysis and politics as these disciplines are rethought, creating knowledges and standpoints that are perhaps necessarily fragmented, built on shifting sands that move towards opening queer politics to different registers of queerness, and other queered languages of *differance*.

My life . . . My life was once very beautiful, like a flower. When I was growing up, I used to think about nothing except studying; studying was everything for my life. To study all the time was something I liked. I used to compete with everyone in studies, they all tried to defeat me, but nobody managed to do so. Since I was very young, I used to study under my grandmother – until class 4. After that, all the years that I have studied have been without tuition classes – I studied by myself. It used to be very difficult, without anyone's help . . . every so often I felt I won't study. But I couldn't stop studying. When I used to study, there was a lot of poverty at home. We could not gather enough food for ourselves. Baba and Ma used to fish in the river . . . Whatever fish they caught and sold that money was used to buy rice. In this meager way we managed our expenses. Sometimes I would go to catch fish with Baba and Ma. Whatever money I would get, I used to keep with myself. I used to save that money. With that saved money, I would buy books, notebooks; I would satisfy my needs. I would not burden my father. This was because to meet the needs of five brothers and sisters was not possible for Baba. He used to buy good books for my elder sisters, but never managed to send them for tuition classes. Neither my brothers. All five of us have struggled hard to study. Now we are grown up. Since we were young, me and my elder sisters, Ma, all of us have worn others' clothes and spent our days. Even then we were at peace . . . there was happiness. We had everything. I had a strong wish to go very far in my studies, but my luck is bad, that is why I have not managed to study so far.

Swapna's letter, page 1.
Translation mine

2
FRAGMENTARY FIELDS
A map of queer politics in India

Any mapping of a movement is a necessarily difficult task, perhaps one that can only present a history of moments or events that have been contingently fixed during its process. In reality, it seems that boundaries and alliances are always shifting, and there are multiple voices that support and contradict one another that emerge from within movements, giving them a dynamic character. And yet, there is a somewhat ephemeral sense of a unified movement, its frontrunners, and even perhaps its vanguards and gatekeepers. As such, there is no singularity to the history of queer politics in India; the history that emerges in the following pages is, therefore, an incomplete and contingent one. It is a history that is not linear, and has its own investments and divestments. Yet, this history is also a necessary one, for it provides markers, however fleeting, that can help trace the motivations, agendas, and future directions of queer politics.

In writing a history that is always already contingent, perhaps we must begin and end with questions that ask how a movement can be mapped. For example, is a movement defined through its organizations, the issues it considers vital, the number of people it impacts, or something else? Which organizations come to be seen as part of the movement, and which do not? Which issues are considered issues at stake, and which ones are considered secondary? Do we study a movement by containing it within a time and space? While these questions can be seen as those pertaining to the very nature of activism or political movements, other questions emerge regarding the process of studying a movement. What material does one rely on to map a movement – minutes from meetings organizations have conducted, pamphlets and posters passed around at political rallies or public gatherings, interviews from people who are part of those organizations, or something else? In other words, *what is the archive of political activism?*

Perhaps these questions remain, to a large extent, contested terrains as the very nature of politics seems to elude any accurate or encompassing definition because the dynamism of the political field disallows every possibility of fixing a meaning that does not produce its own erasures and reifications. Another possibility is that the modes in which we have hitherto tried to approach the political with respect to activism has foreclosed possibilities of engaging with it in ways that are non-reductive. To think in this direction seems to imply that something is evading us in our examination of the political field; whether this displacement occurs between the individual and the political, or is about a shift in the registers of meaning (between the theoretical and the political, or in the realm of language), or both, is uncertain. The former can be seen as a question of essence perhaps, or ontology, while the latter can perhaps be understood as a question of epistemology; as such, both feed into each other and contribute to how we understand politics and its discursive productions.

For example, previous research on women's movements in India has, it seems, focused on the content of its politics while trying to create mappings organized around the issues that are at stake (Gandhi & Shah, 1992), various time periods into which the movements could be classified (Kumar, 1997), and around themes that address the woman's question (Zubaan, 2006; John, 2008). Throughout these texts, the difficulty of mapping activism or any kind of political movement reveals itself. The moment texts circumscribe a boundary for their enquiry, they open themselves to questions of inclusivity. While these texts manage to presence the woman or the woman's truth (where violence, health, literacy, work, etc. become aspects of a woman's life on the basis of which she is discriminated against in a world where relations and positions are patriarchal), they fall prey to the question – which woman's truth is being represented? As such, critiques of women's movements in India have come from the side of Dalit women, who claim that the woman in question is by default an upper caste Hindu woman (Guru, 1995; Rege, 1998; 2006). The question of including disabled women (Ghai, 2002; 2005; Sen, 2016), thinking of mental health as a feminist issue (Davar, 1999), and respecting sex worker rights have all been challenges to the imagination of womanhood within women's movements. Critiques also emerge from the side of lesbian and queer women, who state that the woman in question is always heterosexual at best, and devoid of sexuality at worst (Shah, 2005; Menon, 2007; Dave, 2012). Similar critiques have also been made about feminist movements elsewhere in the world, and perhaps they are inevitable as long as we think of politics in terms of *what* we need to achieve, rather than *how* we can achieve it. It is possible that an ontological approach to politics that is rooted strongly in demarcating which issues are feminist ones remains exclusionary if it does not consider what it means to occupy a feminist position, or how to live a feminist life (Ahmed, 2017), which are epistemological concerns that link the subject to politics.

However, these critiques have become complicated over time, with questions of inclusion and exclusion becoming porous and contested ones, primarily because just as it does not seem possible to claim any universal truth about a political movement, it does not seem possible to claim a universal critique either. Just as mapping the women's movement in India is a difficult project fraught with many challenges, mapping the field of queer politics in India is similarly complicated. The complexity of the various strands at work with respect to queer politics in India makes it almost impossible to provide a fully representative and accurate layout of its terrain. Further, since queer politics seems to have a relatively recent emergence in India, previous attempts at writing its history have been few, with most of them claiming local knowledges or positions that restrict themselves to a particular geographical region, issue, or identity. What I attempt in the following pages is one narrative among many, which tries to follow the trajectory of disagreements and solidarities within queer politics in India based on previous literature, as well as my work with lesbian-bisexual-transmen (henceforth, LBT) collectives across Kolkata, Mumbai, and Bengaluru.

I. Between gender and sexuality

It is more or less agreed upon that what can be called queer politics in India today emerged in the late 1980s and early 1990s, even though the term 'queer' gained currency much later. Homosexuality in general, and the gay male subject in particular, was first addressed as transnational shifts around health raised the issue of HIV/AIDS in India and saw gay men as a population at risk. According to Narrain and Bhan (2005), "[t]he first recorded queer protest in India was organized by the AIDS Bhedbhav Virodhi Andolan (ABVA) [founded in 1989], which took place in 1992, when a rally was organized in Delhi against police harassment of gay men" (p. 9). The lesbian woman as a figure of resistance first emerged in the late 1990s, in response to the Shiv Sena's attack on the film *Fire*. A group of people coalesced into the *Campaign for Lesbian Rights* (*Caleri*), and "[t]he individuals and groups who met after the protests decided to develop a year-long activist effort aimed at pushing forward the issue of lesbian rights at the level of the people, through a public campaign" (*Caleri*, 1999, p. 4). It is not that the gay or lesbian subject did not exist in India prior to these protests, but that the protests shifted the figure of the gay and lesbian subject from a relatively hidden and obscure position in the Indian imaginary to a more public one. Perhaps the first lesbian collective to emerge in India was *Sakhi*, a group formed in 1991 in Delhi. Dave (2012) documents how *Sakhi* emerged in relation to an autonomous women's group in Delhi; around the same time, *Stree Sangam* (now *LABIA*) emerged in relation to another autonomous women's group in Bombay (now Mumbai) – the *Forum against Oppression of Women* (FAOW) in 1995.

Already it is apparent that groups, organizations, or collectives that belong within the larger ambit of queer politics in India appear to have emerged from different histories. It seems that gay men in India coalesced together to resist police atrocity that carried the baggage of discrimination on the basis of health and unsafe sex, whereas the lesbian woman subject in India emerged in public in response to attacks on Deepa Mehta's *Fire* (Basu, 2006). This difference in their emergent positions seemed to impact the trajectories of their politics and determined their agendas in the future. While gay rights mostly worked with the discourse linking disease and sexuality, health and safety, lesbian women began their journeys largely from within women's movements, where women were inaugurating the question of sexuality, and through sexuality, different imaginations of a gendered body. The Indian woman was no longer only heterosexual, and by calling her implicit heterosexuality into question, lesbian rights also attempted to open up discussions in the women's movement around women's lives that did not take the usual trajectory of marriage and reproduction, arguably expanding the concept of 'Woman' in the process.

Lesbian sexuality and the women's movement: convergences and resistances

Because the women who made up the early groups and collectives of the queer movement in India were mostly associated with autonomous women's groups of the 1980s, they were attempting to examine gender and sexuality in intersectional ways. According to Shah (2005), her "political understanding of why society was the way it was grew with a composite understanding of how gender, class and caste affected its institutions and structures" (p. 144), and just as her involvement in the women's movement affected her configurations of queerness, queer "lives started forcing a space within the larger women's movements as well" (Ibid., p. 145). While these discussions had begun to take place in the late 1980s and early 1990s, it was the advent of *Fire* in 1998 and the agitations against the film that irrevocably highlighted the question of lesbianism, such that it "clearly fractured [the] legacy of Indian womanhood, and, indeed, of Indian feminism" (John & Niranjana, 2000, p. 372).

For others who were involved in queer activism in the 1990s, the turn to feminism and the women's movements in India was a natural step, since lesbianism was for them, first and foremost, a women's issue. According to Shah (2005), "[t]he women's movements were the first to articulate concern over the control over sexuality and the societal constructions of gender and are hence the closest link and support for the nascent 'queer' movements in the country" (p. 153). The problems the women's movements were raising at the time, around violence against women, rights to land, and their position as labouring women, were seen as connected to the question of sexuality. Lesbian sexuality, or queer sexuality, was something that deeply impacted a woman's life, especially since it seemed to break the silence around a woman's desire and body, inaugurating a new dynamic of how gendered oppression could be understood.

However, even as early groups or collectives who had begun to talk about non-heterosexual desire among women turned to women's movements for support, the relationship began rather tenuously. While counter-heteronormative movements thought of women's movements as their natural ally, many from that space were initially openly homophobic, and later, discretely so (Menon, 2007). Dave (2012) attempts an analysis of why sexuality was always 'less urgent' than other issues that came to occupy the attention of women's movements, and according to her, as the Indian economy opened up to external market forces in 1991, women's movements had to take on board the question of economy in earnest as the gap between upper- and middle-class women's activists and the subjects of their activism, i.e., rural women, began to widen. In Dave's reading, the nature of women's movements was shifting to forms of activism that increasingly relied on non-governmental organizations (henceforth, NGOs), which, because of transnational pressures of funding, did not allow women's movements to take on the question of lesbian sexuality directly. As autonomous groups began to focus on issues of rape and domestic violence, it became important for allied groups (especially those allied with Left politics) to focus on class concerns. As a result, these conditions led women's movements to think of "lesbian sexuality as a matter of indulgence . . . and as private rather than social" (Dave, 2012, p. 103). In a similar interpretation of women's rights groups claiming to be supportive of lesbianism by calling it 'a personal choice' in the aftermath of *Fire*, *Caleri*'s dossier makes it clear that this is an "unfortunate and demeaning dismissal" (*Caleri*, 1999, p. 19) of lesbian lives, simply "homophobia trying to dress itself in liberal drag" (Ibid., p. 19). This succeeded in isolating the issue of lesbian sexuality to a small minority of women, allowing women's movements to claim that it was not as urgent an issue as questions of land and labour that impact a larger group of women.

Behind this logic that centred on the role of changing economy on the Indian woman, there was, according to Dave (2012), an argument for cultural protectionism and gendered essentialism. When, in 1994, Vimla Faroqui (head of the National Federation of Indian Women at the time) wrote a letter to the Prime Minister opposing homosexuality because it was an inherited Western vulgarity that was a direct result of the liberalization policies adopted by the government in 1991, her actions revealed how "[t]he women's movement's politics of class and nationality in a liberalizing economy worked to shape and delimit lesbian politics emerging with it" (Dave, 2012, p. 122). As a result, those talking of lesbian sexuality had to tactically use examples of violence and brutality, especially by highlighting lesbian suicides, in order to evoke affective urgency and transcend the bias that queer sexuality was strictly a middle- and upper-class phenomenon (see Chapter 4). However, this tactic seemed to displace the importance of sexuality to highlight other forms of oppression. Under such conditions, a rural lesbian suicide is perhaps read as important because sexuality is demonstrating its oppression in a situation of poverty, rather than sexuality being seen as a significant part of feminism by itself. Dave's (2012) analysis of the link between an openly homophobic position and a covert homophobia that reveals itself through the dilution of a direct approach towards queer sexualities is extremely pertinent. Perhaps because of the way in which discourses around sexuality have proliferated, albeit under the delusion of being so close to the civilizational taboo (Foucault,

1978; John & Nair, 1998), it must always be an issue that is slightly displaced by considerations of gender, economy, globalization, colonialism, kinship, and so on. While acknowledging that sexuality is not a product of any kind of discursive vacuum, and while highlighting that socio-cultural questions and dynamics of political economy are vital to any understanding of sexuality, it is still important to ask – *when is it a good time to talk about (queer) sexuality?*

As time passed, and lesbian sexuality refused to be an issue that could be ignored or opposed, at least within women's movements in India, it seems a kind of tokenism came into play. *Jagori*, an autonomous women's collective in Delhi, opposed Vimla Faroqi's letter claiming that homosexuality was a matter of human rights. This response was a way to distance the larger role of feminism and women's movements on issues of queer sexuality, for it diffused the specificity of the question. It seems that inclusion within the women's movement was no longer a predicament for people who were fighting for lesbian sexuality, but the conditions of inclusion were still problematic. A founder of *Sappho for Equality*, talking of membership of a women's rights organization in West Bengal, says, "officially we became members . . . But once you do [become a member], whether your voice will be addressed or not was a million dollar question" (Personal correspondence, November, 2015). Another member, discussing membership of the same women's rights organization says, "there was no exchange, conflict, or coming together of any standpoint, I think" (Personal correspondence, 2015).

These overt conflicts or covert detachments, coupled with the urgency that was felt in the aftermath of *Fire*, led to the creation of a number of lesbian and bisexual women's groups across India. It was finally time to come out into the open. One of the reasons for *Caleri*'s formation, in their own words, was the difficulty they experienced with women's movements. Around this time, *Sangini* (Delhi) emerged as a lesbian group in 1997, in addition to the existing *Stree Sangam* (Mumbai), and *Caleri* (Delhi) joined soon afterwards in 1998. *Sappho* (Kolkata) came into existence in 1999 (branching out into *Sappho for Equality* in 2003), and *OLAVA* (Organized Lesbian Alliance for Visibility and Action) came into being in 2000. Within a few years of *Fire*, lesbian and bisexual women had coalesced into numerous groups, organizations, and collectives, each with its own agendas but perhaps all driven with the same sense of urgency: they had realized that the time had finally come to make their presence felt in Indian society, and silence would no longer protect them (*Caleri*, 1999). As more lesbian and bisexual women began to make themselves heard, queer sexuality became an issue that began to be raised repeatedly in the Indian imaginary, with or without the support of women's organizations.

However, the situation was not quite so bleak, and relations between the women's movement and those working on lesbian sexuality were not always only fragile. Those working on lesbian and bisexual sexuality refused to give up their roots in women's movements as a strategic move, and demonstrated how unsafe such spaces actually were (Shah, 2005). Their persistent presence and refusal to be ignored was met by an ability of women's movements to be reflexive, and to include newer imaginations of sexuality and caste within their political imaginations over time. In the 5th National Conference on Women's Movements in India (henceforth, NCWM), held in Tirupati in 1994, verbal disagreements on whether to include lesbian sexuality as a women's movement issue led to some activists demanding that the NCWM pass an anti-lesbian resolution (Dave, 2012). In response, lesbian and bisexual women and women who were in relationships with women or attracted to them but did not identify as lesbian or bisexual in attendance held a meeting during the conference that was only open to non-heterosexual women (Menon, 2007). Even in this meeting, it was clearly documented that women who were dissenting against lesbianism were minority voices. The 7th NCWM, held in Calcutta in 2006, saw in attendance transgender women, women who were sex workers, and lesbian and bisexual women, where sex work and gender and sexualities were given their own panels as a move towards inclusion and diversity. Since then, the Indian Association of Women's Studies (IAWS) has also passed resolutions against Section 377 (Menon, 2007).

While some spaces of contention remain in the relation between the women's movement and queer activism in India, solidarities seem to have improved with time. It is problematic to see women's movements as a monolith, and therefore, it cannot be claimed that women's movements as a whole were homophobic, especially since some/many lesbian, bisexual, and queer women saw themselves as a part of women's movements. In the dispute between gender and sexuality, as time has passed, more and more efforts are being undertaken to hyphenate the two in a productive relation that moves both sides of activism in newer directions, bringing forth a more productive politics. Feminists have come to claim how lesbian sexuality is an integral part of their struggle, and how questioning the norm of heterosexuality is useful for feminism in order to destabilize the hierarchy of gender and sexuality (John & Nair, 1998;

Menon, 2007). Some queer activists, on their part, have refused to part with their feminist roots, which has brought them into disagreements with gay rights activism since its very inception.

The un-ease of gender in queer politics: one reading of Section 377

Since the trajectory of politics was very different (although not unrelated) for gay men and lesbian and bisexual women, it seems that their agendas were different from the very inception of their activisms. According to Shah (2005):

> We also tried consistently to ally and work with others in the extended 'sexual minorities' community (which was slowly emerging as the alphabet soup LGBTKQHE . . .) – the gays, the kothis, the hijras . . . Many of their lives and realities were very different from ours. Their issues were more related to public spaces, ours were about invisibility. We were trying to find a community with them – a community which believed in looking at our collective issues and lives within the frameworks of a politics akin to ours. A politics that dealt with injustice, violence, discrimination across all divisions of society, that moved further with vision of a new world. We were not always successful.
>
> (p. 149)

While gay men and lesbian and bisexual women were simultaneously talking about sexuality, and were taking stands away from heterosexuality, they were doing so in very different ways. For queer women, it seems that the starting point of their activism was already informed by an approach to gender that was aware of, and sensitive to, the inequalities perpetuated by patriarchal principles that made a woman the 'second sex'. As such, lesbian and bisexual women often felt that gay men were unable to recognize how patriarchy was oppressive to women, and repeated those same relations of oppression themselves.

Especially for queer women who emerged from women's movements, to witness such patriarchal bias in the gay community was a serious predicament, perhaps one that helped consolidate lesbian and bisexual groups and collectives even further. Stories run rampant even now among such collectives about how gay men often treat lesbianism and bisexuality as an issue that is secondary to their own. Perhaps it is the difference in perspectives that creates too large a chasm to bridge between gay men and lesbian and bisexual women. It is, in other words, the difference of gender, or sexual difference, that does not allow for the issue of their sexuality to come together.

The rootedness of lesbian, bisexual, and queer women in feminism has also led to other ideological disagreements between gay rights activism and lesbian and bisexual collective agendas. One such difference had been around the issue of Section 377 of the Indian Penal Code, which states that any sexual involvement against the order of nature with any man, woman, or animal is punishable by imprisonment. *ABVA* was the first activist group that had begun to challenge the constitutionality of Section 377 in 1994, which was taken up by *Naz Foundation* and *Lawyers Collective* in 2001. The initial problem with Section 377 was seen in the way it became a legal support for the police to harass gay men. The larger discourse around Section 377 was steeped in the HIV/AIDS rhetoric of those times as the groups that began to first question the validity of Section 377 were involved in promoting safe sex among gay men, hijras, and transgender sex workers.

The argument around Section 377, which eventually brought many queer activist groups together, began with contentions that seem to have emerged along the lines of gender. As activists hoping for the overturning of Section 377 began to claim that the nature of sexual activity between two consenting adults in a bedroom was a private affair, and should not be a constitutional issue, feminists in the queer movement raised their problems with such an argument because it promoted a discourse that positioned domestic abuse as a private matter, not relevant for legal redressal. In this fracture along the lines of gender when it came to the rights of asserting one's sexuality, the division between gay men and lesbian women seemed very clear.

A lot has changed over the years, and gay men and lesbian women have come to form political alliances, most notably *PRISM* and *Voices against 377*, which were known to have queer women in roles of leadership. More recently, after the Supreme Court verdict recriminalizing Section 377, the group of people that came together to form *No Going Back* (a fundraising initiative against Section 377 inspired by movements in USA and UK) were a coalition that saw queer people of many orientations and identifications come together. Even though the issue of Section 377 had divided gay men and lesbian and bisexual women, they have come together since then and Section 377 has captured a large part of the queer political imaginary in India (Narrain & Gupta, 2011).

It certainly seems that struggles around law, particularly Section 377, have been an essential feature of queer politics in India. According to Narrain (2007a), "[e]ver since the emergence of queer articulation in the Indian context, there has been a focus on Section 377 as the locus of oppression of the diverse groups which make up India's sexuality minorities" (p. 255). Consequently, Section 377 has contributed significantly in the shaping of queer activism's agendas, and its drives and directions since 1994. According to Narrain (2007b), "the emerging gay and lesbian communities paradoxically owe much to the operation of provisions such as Section 377 of the Indian Penal Code" (p. 52). It is indeed undeniable that Section 377 has been used to commit numerous and variant atrocities against queer persons in India (PUCL-K, 2001), and an argument can be made that its operationalization and presence in Indian governance means more than the cumulative impact of arrests it leads to, or even the unlawful atrocities that are committed under its jurisdiction. According to Narrain and Bhan (2005), the presence of Section 377 leads to an inability to form a national symbolic imagination of non-reproductive heterosexuality, and as such, can be seen as a formidable barrier queer politics in India must cross over. The larger problem with the existence of Section 377 is that it implicates socio-cultural mores, traditions, and morality within law while trying to hold on to its impartial and just nature. This leads to there being "no discourses about queer people in society other than the prejudices, myths and misconceptions that have been perpetuated by the existence of Section 377" (Narrain, 2007b, p. 56).

II. Queer politics of a Third World (post)colony

Insofar as queer politics in India is related to sexuality, and sexuality can be seen as a historical and socio-cultural question that determines subjectivity, queer politics in India cannot be thought of without its relation to India's position as a Third World country with a developing economy, nor can it be thought through without an engagement with India's colonial history. It has been argued that queer politics in India has been significantly impacted by the politics of transnational funding, and to receive or eschew such funding has been a deeply contentious issue within queer politics. Further, the politics of transnational funding has come to be imbricated in the ways in which discourses around hijras, kothis, Men who have Sex with Men (MSM), jogappas, aravanis, and others, have constructed them as 'indigenous' and supplementary genders and sexualities since the 1990s, while genders and sexualities that don't align with globalized identifiers are simultaneously facing erasure (Gross, 2017). This has led to a questioning of the taxonomies of gender/sexuality that are deployed as a result of queer politics in India, particularly as identities. We can perhaps state that the focus of transnational funding and queer politics has been the prevention of HIV/AIDS and the battle against Section 377, and it is here that the questions of transnational history and political economy can be seen to be imbricated with socio-cultural aspects of queer genders and sexualities.

Queer activism's globalized developmentality

The disagreements around Section 377 were not only about the different gendered approaches to sexuality that perhaps came to mark queer politics in India, but also about the ways in which gender differences already existed within members of what would eventually come to be known as the queer community in India. This was related to how Section 377 became implicated in the politics of transnational funding within the field of queer politics in India (Dave, 2012). Gender differences were also made acute since the issue of HIV/AIDS prevention received immense funding from international agencies, which allowed gay men (and some male-to-female transgenders and hijras) to organize in large numbers, whereas funding for issues lesbian and bisexual women worked on were scant (Cohen, 2005; khanna, 2007; Menon, 2007). It seems that the expansion of influence and power resulting from transnational funding created a divide between those who were caught within its discourse, and those who were not included inside its discursive field. It might be possible that lesbian and bisexual women, for whom their invisibility in Indian society was a primary reason behind their politics, were feeling further invisiblized by their queer comrades and allies.

The tensions of transnational funding also highlight the way in which queer politics in India has come to be embroiled in the politics of globalization, and many believe that this history of queer politics is inseparable from the rise of neoliberal agendas in the Indian subcontinent (Dave, 2012; Sircar & Jain, 2017). The division between NGOs that garnered influence on the basis of HIV/AIDS monies, and the groups who could not or did not want to claim these funds was also, therefore, about a difference in ideologies that was linked to relationships with the State, as well as the productions and erasures inherent in development logic. For some, especially those who had a history of involvement in women's movements, to receive funds from organizations that propagated a skewed and orientalist idea of development in a model that demonstrated the superiority of the First World and posited the Third World as lacking was to be complicit in a politics of development that made objects out of Third World subjects and oriented them towards a path where progress was mapped based on First World criteria (Achuthan, 2001). Within this logic, power, meaning, and value are all skewed in favour of the First World, on the side of the White subject who will save the Brown subject from their abjectness, and further still, this imbalance at the very heart of development logic is invisiblized through a naturalization that is a consequence of globalized and neoliberal agendas (Spivak, 1988).

Developmentality and neoliberalism have their own discursive productions and circuits of power that are closely tied to global and cultural capital that sets the Western Subject as the ideal to strive for. As the years have passed, it has been claimed that queer politics in India has come closer to the rights based activism that is characteristic of Western liberalism (Kavi, 2007), which has reduced the promise of what queer politics in India could look like (Dave, 2012); it has come closer and closer to the straight line of developmentality that flows from the First World to the Third World. Funding has created a politics of inclusions, exclusions, and normativities within queer activism, which hint at processes akin to homonationalism. Some groups have split away from each other in light of these differences and the way in which power determines inclusions and ideology in groups that benefit from transnational funding.

The processes of globalization and neoliberalism have shaped not only alliances in queer politics, but also the nature of collectives and the way they have evolved since the 1990s in India. While many lesbian and bisexual groups and collectives had emerged in the 1990s primarily as emotional support groups, the nature of collectives and what collectivization meant has changed over time. Members from *LABIA*, a feminist queer collective working with lesbian and bisexual women and transpersons, describe how the use of the internet to find queer people and communities diffuses the need for groups like theirs to be emotional support groups, allowing them to become a politically charged space with its own agendas and ideologies. A coming together because of their gender and/or sexuality is no longer, it seems, the primary force that binds members of *LABIA*, and other such collectives, together.

Similarly, *Sappho for Equality*, a group that works for lesbian and bisexual women and transmen, also saw itself shift and orient its agendas towards awareness and intervention over the years. In the aftermath of

Fire, six women had created *Sappho*, an emotional support group for lesbian and bisexual women that met on the last Sunday of every month to share their joys, fears, difficulties, and ambitions. Eventually they became *Sappho for Equality*, a group that was politically oriented and eventually came to include transmen and people who were sympathizers of the cause, in addition to lesbian and bisexual women. As the nature of the group evolved, the membership of the group evolved as well. The nature of meetings, conversations, and agendas of the early days also changed over time. From a space that held the precious weight of anxieties and solidarities of lesbian and bisexual women finding their way in the world and discovering their own relation to their sexualities and bodies, *Sappho for Equality* is now a NGO that undertakes projects, produces documentaries, and does significant outreach in West Bengal and its neighbouring states. For some members, this change has been a positive one, while for others it has meant that their own affects and agendas with regard to queer politics have undergone transformations. Perhaps it is not that an argument can be made to preserve that which is now nostalgic, a kind of activism perhaps possible only in the past, but that there is a politics behind the shifting nature of activism over time. It is this politics that needs to be focused on to see how queer activism has transformed over time, simultaneously resignifying meanings of queerness in the process.

While the shift in the nature of *LABIA*, and *Sappho*'s transition to *Sappho for Equality*, took place around the same time, in the early 2000s, it does not seem that both groups transformed in the same way. The most acute difference lies in how *Sappho* and *Sappho for Equality* are related, such that *Sappho* still remains as (a largely defunct) emotional support group, with *Sappho for Equality* as its larger, more actively political sister space. All members of *Sappho* are members of *Sappho for Equality* by default, but it is not so the other way around. This is because *Sappho* remains a group only for lesbian, bisexual, and transmasculine identified persons, while *Sappho for Equality* has a membership regardless of sexual orientation and gender identification. This duality, some argue, maintains the divide between 'un-political' affect and 'political' rationality, between 'private' struggles and 'public' engagements (Roy, 2015). This must be unpacked further. *LABIA* does not host such a duality, which can arguably be a false dichotomy, and it seems that emotions and affect are negotiated within their political space of meetings and interactions. Another organization that works with lesbian and bisexual women and transmasculine persons, *LesBit*, has an entirely different mode of functioning, seemingly circumventing this debate of globalized transitions and the dichotomy of affect and politics by meeting strictly based on need. *LesBit* members, while connected to each other constantly, meet only for specific purposes, such as interventions, or issue based projects.

It cannot be denied that globalization and neoliberalism have produced differences; there have been sides taken over whether transnational funding is acceptable to the way in which queer politics will progress over time, or whether the transnational subject it will produce will be too far removed from what queer subjects imagine themselves and their politics to be. But it seems to also have produced some solidarities, in the way in which queer people have become more accessible to each other, have built a community that is often more virtual than real, and in that sense, more diffuse, more diverse. At this juncture, it might be useful to ask which subjects have been able to reap the benefits of neoliberalism, and at what costs. Has neoliberalism created shifts that have come to determine how different queer subjects are positioned unevenly on the grounds of queer politics? It might be productive to engage with the nature of the change itself, the logic of globalization and neoliberalism as these phenomena interacted with the terrains of queer politics in India. Perhaps we can ask what these processes have done to transform the queer subject in India, and the differences among queer subjectivities based on where they intersect with globalization and neoliberalism, to what degree and effect, and how they are impacted by transnational funding.

The politics of naming and the doubt of cultural difference

If we believe that neoliberal and globalized agendas create a contestation of cultures that swings in the favour of a rhetoric that constantly pushes us to aspire towards whiteness and leads to the production of international and cosmopolitan queer identities (Altman, 1997; 2001; Gross, 2017), one symptom of these seismic shifts can be traced in the production of a taxonomy of terms (Menon, 2007), which become consolidated into identities that eschew the 'local' in favour of the 'global'. The debates over taxonomy – on whether to call the Indian woman who loves women a lesbian or to call the Indian man who loves men gay, and whether they will identify themselves as such – have been persistent questions since the very beginning of what has come to be consolidated as queer activism in India (Dave, 2012). What lies rooted within these debates is a question of cultural specificity, which seems to mark itself with the idea of homosexuality being a Western construct that enters the Indian context after the Indian economy opens up to liberalization. This cultural specificity also takes the form of recourse to Indian traditions, one side of which sees homosexuality as a pollutant to the purity of Indian heritage, while the other side claims that homosexuality has always existed within Indian culture (Thadani, 1996; Vanita & Kidwai, 2008). Somewhere in this matrix of 'Western influences', puritanical Indian traditions, and the erasures and reclamations of history, terms that signify queer sexuality emerge in particular ways.

Dave (2012) demonstrates how *Sakhi* grappled with the need to openly identify as a 'lesbian' collective when it emerged in 1991. This need materialized in a sense of freedom they associated with the identification 'Indian and lesbian'; to claim that one was a 'lesbian' was to counter the belief that the 'Indian woman' could not step outside her assigned gendered and sexed roles. Further, as *Sakhi* began to circulate its post box number, letters came from all across India, demonstrating how it was not only elite and cosmopolitan Indian women who were identifying themselves as lesbians, but women from across economic and geographic boundaries were also doing the same. The media also played a role in eliciting such recognitions as it began to publicize an incident of marriage between two policewomen in the late 1980s – Leela and Urmila, who, however, rejected the term 'lesbian' for themselves.

That *Sakhi* had decided to take a political stance in favour of visibility and public emergence by calling themselves an openly 'lesbian' collective had its own consequences. It meant that they had to distinguish themselves from the spaces of homosociality within a heterosexual world where lesbianism thrived. In this process, *Sakhi* was defining a new kind of lesbian subjectivity, one that was proper and political, at the cost of excluding other homosocial realities that were rampant but secret. This led to the emergence of a new lesbian subject who was not only politically conscious, but also had the cultural capital to state her politics and access the freedom of movement that was required for a collective of lesbian women to meet. This often involved the collective circumscribing itself into a group of urban, middle- or upper-middle-class women who were mostly well educated and independent. While these exclusions were not deliberate, they were perhaps errors of omission that demarcated the outer limits of a field of politics for the Indian lesbian woman, implying that some aspects of her life were political, while others were not.

Some groups or collectives had anticipated these difficulties perhaps, or they thought that identifying as 'lesbian' would efface their Indian-ness in some way. However, as the years progressed, more and more groups and collectives emerged as openly lesbian and/or bisexual. *Caleri* took notice of the exclusion that might be caused by calling themselves 'lesbian' publicly, as it would exclude "rural women and women from the urban poor who don't speak English but lead woman-loving lives" (*Caleri*, 1999, p. 24), but decided that it was more urgent to identify as 'lesbian' at the time. Similar decisions were also made by *Stree Sangam*. The effect of this was that now there seemed to be a clearer understanding of what it meant to *be* a lesbian or bisexual woman. As certain constructions of 'lesbian' or 'bisexual' identity reified, simultaneously the space that obscurity had provided for homosociality slowly eroded as lesbianism became part of public discourse.

As groups and collectives began to become consolidated into demarcated categories of lesbian or bisexual (or for that matter, gay), and as newer members were inducted into these spaces, they seemed to acquire the language in which these groups operated – perhaps a language that was simultaneously a product and productive of these consolidations of identity and subjectivity. It was through their membership in such collectives that they evolved understandings of what it meant to be a 'lesbian' or a 'bisexual' woman, and perhaps it was the resignification of discourses in such spaces that produced very *real* shifts in the signifiers that marked their *subjectivization* as gendered, sexual, and desiring subjects. The gradual entry of the internet in particular, and Western cultural influence in general, now seems to determine the newer queer subject who was coming of age in the 2000s and later, who already knows how to label their own sexual orientation, consumes queer media, helped by queer friendly websites, podcasts, and shows like 'The L Word'. This is also subjectivization and interpellation, albeit one that perhaps produces different subjects than those of the late 1980s and early 1990s.

This is not to claim in any way that various manifestations of queerness are not an Indian phenomenon, but rather that queer subjects with some amount of socio-cultural capital now know how to identify themselves; they are no longer searching for referents and signifiers. The debates of the 1980s and 1990s, where other terms were also being used to signify same-sex desire, no longer seem to be important debates in today's scenario. However, it is also acknowledged that some terms do come with the paleonymic weight of colonialism, or globalization, and the task of decolonization is necessary for the Third World (post)colonial subject if sexuality is to be retrieved from Western logics (Dutta, 2013). One reason for why local terms and phrases that signified queerness could not be used productively in the 1980s and 1990s may be because terms such as *'humjinsi'*, *'khush'*, or *'aisi mahila jo dusri mahilaon ki taraf aakarshith hoti hai'* could not gain the popularity of the term 'lesbian' in the political imaginary; perhaps since queer activism was coming closer to its Western counterparts, the terminologies of the West were easier to claim.

The 'coming out' that became intricately tied to identifying as a 'lesbian' woman, as opposed to identifying with another signifier of queer sexuality, also became an emergent need after attacks on *Fire* in 1998, where nationalism and the purity of the Indian (albeit Hindu) nation was at stake in accepting the love and eroticism between two women. As the *Shiv Sena* and *Bajrang Dal* stopped screenings and vandalized movie theatres, the discourse that emerged was that lesbianism is alien to Indian culture. Despite the fact that many feminists and queer women had critiques of *Fire* (*Caleri*, 1999; Bose, 2007), the political charge with which lesbianism in India was opposed shocked many into resisting invisibility and acting against allegations of queer sexuality being alien to Western culture. When Bal Thackeray claimed that the film would be tolerable if the two women were not Hindu but Muslim, another facet of Indian nationalism revealed itself, seemingly grounded in illicit sexuality and its relation to the Indian nation. Bandyopadhyay (2012) argues that what unravelled as the effect of *Fire* was merely a symptom; the real issue was that *Fire* was an irruptive event that allowed a sexualization of the political scenario – the lesbian, like the Muslim, had to be excluded in order to form the Indian nation. This exclusion emerges through the Law of the Excluded Middle, where a binary is established by suppressing, or repressing, the proximity and sameness of two elements. The sameness, that now lies repressed, produces an excessive reaction when it is confronted. It is this excess that demonstrated itself as reactions to *Fire*, and lesbian women across the country responded by coming together to form various collectives and groups that led the lesbian to emerge as a political figure in later years.

Over the years, the dangers of the link between queer sexuality and nationalism have become even more acute as global shifts that co-opt queer politics in order to create exclusions along the lines of class, caste, race, and religion have become more frequent, giving birth to a politics where queers turn against themselves (Puar, 2007; 2017). Puar (1998) suggests that the goal of 'queer' politics is always inclusion, and that it is complicit in 'exclusionary epistemes' that trade some queer lives for the privileges of queer nationalisms. She claims that genealogies of 'queer' never presence the complexities of the nation-state, and as such it does not take into consideration how it is complicit in the exclusions and inclusions of the nation-state. If we understand the nation-state as a particular form of controls and coercions that maintain a condition of dispossession (Butler & Spivak, 2010), then is queer politics in India also complicit in forgetting the costs of claiming the 'queer' within nationalist folds, rendering invisible those outsided and dispossessed by its borders? In the Indian context, where we are yet to reach the fulfillment of a homonationalist moment, perhaps it is vital to consider what queerness means as it rests on a resignification of sexuality in the colonial past and seems to build on imaginations of an increasingly neoliberal future.

Perhaps at the heart of the tension between queerness, nationalism, and neoliberalism in the Indian context is the question of culture. As lesbianism became the grounds on which the Indian nation seemed to reassert itself in the late 1990s, what the allegations of homosexuality being a Western import could not refuse, perhaps, was that some terms in usage within queer activism today first emerged in the West, 'queer' itself being one of them. This is not to say that homosexuality or same-sex desire did not exist within Indian culture, but that the entry of these terms perhaps shifted the register of what homosexuality meant. Menon (2007) makes an argument that such terms – lesbian, gay, bisexual, transgender, queer – are made possible through an erasure of a history of Indian sexuality, so that terms that were used to describe homosexuality or homo-eroticism are no longer available. As a result of this erasure, there is a strange absence of significations, which is then filled with terms that have histories in and of the West. Bacchetta (2007) argues that this erasure goes beyond that of terminologies and influences how we think of queer politics in India. For her, to see the history of queer politics in India as emerging in the late 1980s and 1990s is to erase its manifestations in the past, an erasure that demonstrates queer politics' complicity with First World orientations.

An erasure of terms is perhaps never a simple erasure. It can also mean an effacement of history, which in turn, can potentially lead to a voiding of the historical subject. What remains, then, or rather, what is produced over time, is a subject subjected to, or subjectivated in (Butler, 1997), a Western term, and a Western logic of sexuality. This subject would not be the same subject of an Indian past, because what would be reconfigured is Indian-ness itself. However, if this theorization of erasure holds, what remains as a question is whether the erasure and consequent contestation of cultures produces a subject that embodies this contestation, with parts of them not easily reclaimable any longer, while other parts of their sexuality, now reconfigured perhaps, find newer articulations. It seems that this subject would be close to a condition or position of subalternity, where parts of their subjectivity would exist as non-things or voids, unable to find representation or signification in current discourses of (queer) sexuality. If such erasures also produce subjects who are unable to embody the contestation of cultures – in other words, subjects who cannot access globalization even if globalization is impacting them – then do these subjects become lost in the void, unable to articulate themselves as queer language mutates, becoming the sexual subaltern subject?

A theorization of the contemporary queer subject in India cannot perhaps be described without engaging with the queer taxonomies that have been created in the past two or three decades via an implosion of terms and meanings. As Narrain and Bhan (2005) explain:

> If one were to compile an *open-ended register* which would reflect some of the *diverse practices* that come under the political project of 'queer', this list would minimally include: The Hijras . . . Kothis . . . Lesbian, Gay, Bisexual, and Transgender Communities (LGBT).
>
> *(p. 5. Emphasis mine)*

It is argued that categories such as MSM, kothi, and panthi emerged only with the arrival of transnational HIV/AIDS funding, which required some articulation of indigenous gender performance and sexual orientation in order to be claimed (Cohen, 2005). Within these classifications are further subdivisions, such as between butch and femme for lesbians, between gay men and MSM, between those who are transgender, transmen, transwomen, or trans★ (a term introduced by *LABIA* in their research project *Breaking the Binary*, in 2013). It seems that terms that come to constitute queer taxonomies have multiplied, and have done so based on the logic of classifying sexual practices and behaviours.

I theorize that such a queer taxonomy emerges in relation to the structures it is excluded from, and consequently, the structures it attempts to resist and change. It emerges, perhaps, in order to represent the various subjects of queer politics (the diversity of sexual practices, then, would ensure the variety of terms used to describing them). As the terms to describe genders and sexualities increase, each term seems to fix its own meaning, as a result of which non-heterosexual subjects are fixed into particular identities. According to Bose and Bhattacharyya (2007): "Any serious study of sexuality/sexualities and the politics perpetually at play in determining the complex, diverse connotations of these terms must necessarily start with a consideration of notions of identity and identity-formation, sexual or otherwise" (p. x). As terms become identities, politics also begins to focus on frameworks around human rights and inclusive citizenship. This politics highlights the experience of marginalization faced by people of non-heterosexual sexualities, who embody their discrimination in their claims towards equal human rights. In this framework of politics, coalitions are formed on the basis of identity, as opposed to being formed in spite of identity. As differences increase between lesbian, gay, bisexual, and transgender groups, as well as within them, the movement is precariously linked in its turn away from the heterosexual norm.

Since the late 1990s and early 2000s, the term 'queer' came to hold the movement together, however unsteady the binds between its various strands might be. Queer politics has, for the most part, emerged in India only in the past decade. During this time, the term 'queer' has been associated with a kind of radical potential that was as if missing from the politics that had hitherto been a result of seemingly grounded identities like lesbian, gay, bisexual, transgender, etc. To be queer has been a matter of personal identity, as well as a conscious political choice. For Narrain and Bhan (2005), to politicize the signifier 'queer' is to imagine it as a rejection of the heterosexual and patriarchal family, and imagine a politics that moves beyond identity and minority to bleed into our very notions of class, gender, sexuality, caste, religion, and so on as inherently intersectional. This potential of blurring the lines between political involvement and personal identity, as well as the possibility of alliances across intersections embodied queer politics with a promise of radical subversion. For Menon (2007), queer politics is that which boycotts universality, perhaps in favour of contingency, holding the potential to subvert not only the heterosexual, patriarchal family, but also the idea of nation and citizenship itself. Queer politics "must be seen as having two dimensions – one, 'over' the nation, across national borders, and two, 'under' the nation, resisting inclusion into the 'larger' national identity" (p. 40). In this simultaneous movement of queer politics 'over' and 'under' the idea of the nation, it would prove itself to be counter-heteronormative, questioning citizenship, democracy, and nationhood.

Queer politics, therefore, becomes broadly about subverting the hetero-patriarchal norm by occupying or embodying radical difference. Including within it various aspects of lesbian, gay, bisexual, and transgender resistance, queer politics seems to go beyond these categorizations and establishes itself as a politics embodying the very difference that was previously the basis of marginalization, in order to reclaim and even celebrate the very aspects of oneself that were seen as pejorative, deviant, or even dangerous. To occupy the term 'queer' was a subversive move that established queer politics as one that derived power from the place of its own oppression. If we believe that, "queer describes those gestures or analytical models which dramatize incoherencies in the allegedly stable relations between chromosomal sex, gender and sexual desire" (Jagose, 1996, p. 3), then it is these very models that are its primary interlocutors. "Resisting that model of stability – which claims heterosexuality as its origin, when it is more properly its effect – . . . [the task of queer politics is to focus] on mismatches between sex, gender, and desire" (Ibid., p. 3). In other words, it is the stable model of heterosexual relations that counters queer subjectivities, and must therefore be encountered by queer politics; queer politics must then *speak to* heterosexuality.

However, there were contestations over the term 'queer' as well. While it had a particular history of emergence in the West, where it was claimed by LGBT activists seeking to reclaim what had, for years, been an insult deployed as a signifier of shame, it did not have the same history of reclamation in India. The term, an affect laden and difficult signifier for LGBT activists of the West, did not perhaps carry the same paleonymic weight of resignification across cultures. It was the radical potential of 'queer'-ness to encompass the different, and often contentious, strands of LGBT activism in an attempt that tried to move away from the fixity of identity and identity politics that was the promise of using 'queer' across trans-nationalities. However, in the travel of a signifier across nations and cultures, perhaps the term could not be used in its full import in the Indian context. As a member of *Sappho for Equality* says, "Sometimes I do feel . . . I am not comfortable with the term queer also . . . because in its aim to include or serve as an umbrella term, or maybe deconstructive term, it is unable to communicate a lot" (Personal correspondence, November, 2015).

Here, one can ask what the weight and import of a term like 'queer' is in an Indian socio-cultural context. While it is true that terms, just like politics or theory, can indeed travel, that process would perhaps also reconfigure its meanings. And so, what history does the term 'queer' carry when it arrives in India, to be used as a radical umbrella term that pushes the boundaries of LGBT politics? Or is it a term that arrives suddenly, without the history of its degradation, a sign that queer politics in India is embracing the paths of its Western counterparts? Does that mean the term 'queer' is a signifier with no corresponding signified, ready to mean different things to different people in diverse circumstances? If so, who can use this term for themselves, claim it without shame, without fear, in pleasure and in pride? And who remains entirely absented from this term, entirely ignorant of it, on whom it will be imposed from an/Other; who cannot claim such a term at all? Further, if queerness is that which is radical, is all queer politics subversive? Where does the radical potential of queer politics lie? What are the ways in which queer politics can subvert existing structures and hierarchies of gender? Does queer politics have a productive imagination of politics that includes the promise of coalition and sidesteps the difficulties of identity politics?

III. Interlude

Could Swapna and Sucheta be placed within these terrains of queer activism? Where would they be situated, as subjects or as objects? Would their lives find articulation, a language in which to speak queerly, clearly? Would they have to claim identity, marginalization, and rights? These questions emerge from a doubt: are Swapna and Sucheta the subjects that queer politics in India attempts to represent? If they are not, will they be asked to learn how to speak to become queer subjects, and unlearn their other tongues? Will they be represented as another lesbian death on record? What will those representations reveal, and what of Swapna and Sucheta might be erased? Are they the subjects who are claimed by the untranslatability of a queer politics in India that meets globalized agendas?

Also, another set of questions: what is *queer* about queer politics in India, and does that queerness accept Swapna and Sucheta within its fold, or does it simply stake its hold on them? Between acceptance and exception, can Swapna and Sucheta speak of themselves and their lives within queer politics in India, within its many strands, its multiple standpoints? Or will they be spoken for by those who already know and articulate the language of queer politics in India? And, in order to answer these questions, to ask another one – who is the subject of queer politics in India, or rather, who is the political subject who transforms queer politics in India?

Perhaps to begin to answer these questions is to delve into the way in which we think of and theorize the political field, as opposed to thinking through the nature of politics. Perhaps, in the shift from ontology to epistemology, which might entail a shift from queer politics to the queer political subject, there will be space not only for reflexivity, but also for attenuation to the process of politics, and the creation of the political subject in relation to such politics. Perhaps, then we must ask different questions, or ask the same questions differently. Maybe the truths that will emerge from this shift will be contingent, contextual, but truths nonetheless . . .

And if these truths are contingent formulations, based on context, between a politics of the present and its difficult relations to histories of the past, what questions must we ask when studying a movement? How must we orient those questions . . . would they be queerly oriented, or seek out oriental queerness?

. . . After my studies stopped, I started giving tuitions. After meeting my basic needs, whatever money remained I used to give at home. During that time, I became very close friends with Durga. We used to like-love each other a lot. One day, her marriage was fixed. I celebrated a lot during her wedding. But, even now there has been nothing wrong between her and me. After that, I used to spend a lot of time with Phalguni. During that time, Tina was my friend. I used to like-love them a lot. They also used to like-love me a lot. Even now, they do. If you like-love someone, it is possible to like-love them forever. To see them, or speak to them, is not necessary. That I like-love, is itself important. Many things have happened in my life, and even if I start to tell the stories, I will never manage to say it all. In the middle, I was alone. I used to travel alone; it felt nice to be alone. I used to stay by myself, the way I wanted to. After that, Such (Sucheta) and I started talking a little. I used to meet Such's elder sister a lot. Because of that, I used to go to their pond to bathe. Because of that, I used to be very close to both of them. After that, Such's elder sister got married. Then, Such used to spend time with me, talk to me. She was very naughty then. She used to do whatever she felt like doing. She used to joke around with me, and would make me laugh frequently. I used to scold her a lot. She would go away. She would argue with me, she never used to listen. After that, I used to like-love her a lot. Slowly, talking to her, meeting her increased. After that, she likes-loves me a lot . . . I also like-love her a lot, even more than my own life. But I don't know why. But when I didn't see her, didn't talk to her, I used to feel sad. She used to feel the same way. She herself also liked-loved me a lot. She herself also likes-loves me a lot, maybe even more than me.

Swapna's letter, page 2.
Translation mine

3
QUEER/POLITICAL/SUBJECT

In the previous chapter, I attempted to trace one kind of history of queer politics in India where feminist queer or queer feminist perspectives were represented over others. The rooted and related nature of LBT collectives with the women's movement in India, and the acrimonious but productive relations with gay activist organizations that work with HIV/AIDS funding are two strands through which their alliances and political imaginations have been explored, and I have tried to place these relations alongside questions of how queer politics in India shapes, and is shaped by, culture, neoliberalism, (post)colonialism, and globalization. In this chapter, I'd like to turn to the queer political subject, assuming that such a subject is placed in some relation, however obliquely, within the topology of queer politics. To question this assumption, we must perhaps define what 'queer' means, and demarcate a boundary for what is political and apolitical about queerness. The previous chapter traced how lesbian and bisexual women's collectives began to appear in the late 1980s and early 1990s, and how their constitution led to such a division by default, where some women were 'political', while others were not. Here, I would like to contend that this division itself reveals something about queer politics. Who is seen as a legitimate, political, and 'good' queer subject, and who is framed as an illegitimate, apolitical, and 'bad' queer subject is also about how queer politics demarcates its field and its reach, and who it includes and excludes.

While I would not like to mark a good or bad queer figure in this work, perhaps we cannot say that such divisions are unnecessary; all acts by queer people may not be 'queer', just like all women are not, by default, feminists. We must therefore think through what it means to *be* 'queer', to *do* 'queer' things, to *embody* 'queerness', and to demarcate a difference and overlap between such being, doing, and embodiment. But it seems that until we can reach a point of agreement in such debates, or formulate a queer standpoint, however provisional, it might be premature to create this division. Behind this particular assumption lies a possibility that not all persons representing queer activism are necessarily embodiments of queerness, and may not have a productive relation with doing queer things, while those subjects such representation misses out on, erases, or objectifies, might show us newer ways to *queer* what we imagine queer politics to be.

In this chapter, I would like to focus on the processes that bestow legitimacy to certain queer subjects at the expense of others, and try to follow the trajectories that relate queer subjects who come to represent or author queer politics with queer subjects who are effaced or obfuscated by queer politics while remaining subjected to its dynamics. This perhaps necessitates a move beyond thinking of queer politics in terms of geographical boundaries or ideological terrains in order to explore the drives, directions, and motivations of queer politics; it is to think through what queer politics wants, as opposed to how queer politics manifests itself. To do so is also to remain imbricated in questions that link queerness, power, and resistance. In other words, what does it mean to be queer? Where, within the frame of politics, does resistance lie, and how does resistance frame politics; what is the link between politics and transformation, and how can this transformation be defined – on which axis can transformation be mapped? What would it mean to do politics queerly, in a way that it cannot be co-opted by power? And then, who finds their actions classified as politics? Who is the subject of queer politics, or the queer political subject, and who is subjected to queer politics?

I. The political subject of queer politics

Samaddar (2010) writes about the conditions of emergence of a political subject who authors politics while simultaneously being a subject of politics; such a subject emerges through the function of a collective, with the *desire* to resist power by acting like a *supplement*, which emphasizes that something of this subject works to escape or exceed being defined by political systems, legal codifications, and power structures. Such a subject has an agenda that is formed on the basis of ideas about transformation, and is a material, or bodily subject, in that politics is enacted through and upon its body. Samaddar calls this subject a 'citizen-militant', "less of a citizen because s/he has either opted out, or s/he has not been taken in as a legitimate member of the political society" (Ibid., p. xix). In this framework, the political subject *resists* on a different register of meaning to its opposition, speaking in a language that is untranslatable by what it opposes; as such, its resistance cannot be co-opted by the discourse it acts against. Perhaps it is this untranslatability, this shift in registers between power and resistance, which gives the political subject its function of excess, as if slipping away from meaning; this is a subject that can never be fully understood, and therefore assimilated, by power.

Reading the two opposing sides as that of power and resistance, Samaddar's political subject emerges in a dialectic between the two, and as such, is a result of constant contradictions. The political subject emerges against an already existing structure or system, and carries with it an alternative imagination of transformation. Such a subject is able to create new forms of political life, expanding what politics means, but also maintains older forms of political life, insofar as its opposition is directed towards such systems and structures. This process leads to a resignification of what we understand as politics, or the political, where "the political is within the im-political, making the im-political *inclined* to return to politics. It is in this perpetual oscillation that the political subject finds itself" (Ibid. p. 8). These oscillations not only build collectivity, but also reopen closures or aporias and bring them into the political field as grounds for engagement. In such a view of the political subject, politics itself embodies a split nature, between sovereignty and resistance, between truth and untruth, between death and dialogue, between power and desire, and between the subject and the State. Here, politics, as well as the political subject, are functions of the 'in between'; in other words, they occupy the split, contrariness, and contradiction in a way in which they are simultaneously created by such a split while creating the split. This is to locate the field of politics and the political subject as (im)possibility, always at the border-zones of two tendentious positions in overdetermined relations with each other.

Within this framework, resistance is that which is not seduced by power, that which does not desire power, and as such, has its own articulation and language that does not speak the language of the State. Political resistance becomes something that cannot be co-opted, for the register of resistance is that of desire, not power. Here, the political subject desires transformation, a concrete change in existing structures, systems, and discourses of power. This generates a dialectic between power (the State) and desire (the political subject) that then must lead to contradictions and incomplete translations in the discourse of actions, which finally produces a mutation, the generation of something new that can no longer be explained by either power or desire alone. Such an imagination of the political subject may be useful in understanding the subject of queer politics, perhaps in order to locate the desire of such subjects and to articulate what queer resistance might look like.

The queer legal subject and identity

In the previous chapter, I tried to demonstrate how early discourses against Section 377 disagreed on whether to frame it as a public or private matter (Narrain, 2007b; Dave, 2012; Ailawadi, 2014). Over time, these differences gave way for a mostly unified queer movement that was driven towards the removal of Section 377, and through that, aimed for inclusive and equal citizenship. However, it can also be said that the battle for Section 377 has taken place at the cost of undervaluing other laws that are used to discriminate against some sections of queer people, such as the Immoral Traffic Prevention Act (ITPA) that is used against transgender and MSM sex workers. It can be argued that Section 377 and the discourse of its resistance have erased the figures of the lesbian and hijra as representatives of queer subjectivity in India, while imposing its importance on them insofar as they are subjects of queer politics. Further, khanna (2016) demonstrates how advocating against Section 377 has increased the number of cases where it is used by the police to penalize queer persons, primarily because advocacy allowed it to proliferate into public discourse. In fact, many queer activists feel that the removal of Section 377 will not pave the way for better conditions of living for queer people, and are wary of the impact of legal reform in the collective conscious of queer politics in India. Yet, there are others who argue that legal reform plays a greater role in queer politics, and is linked to transformation of society and culture on a symbolic level (Narrain, 2007a), an argument that is an inheritance of the women's movements in India (Narrain, 2007b).

For Samaddar (2010), perhaps the pull of the law is an inevitable one for any movement that attempts to resist the State, while the State uses the law to morph resistance into something that can fit within its discourses and produce law abiding, conditionally included citizens. In doing so, the

State manages to shift the register of signification within which resistance operates and co-opts it, diluting its meaning, and possibly, the impact of its politics. This dialectic between the State and the political subject raises certain questions. For example, does this dialectic necessarily have to take place within a discourse of the demand for (equal) rights? If so, what does the rights discourse do to the political subject, its imaginations of the future, and its desire for resistance? Does the granting of certain rights take the political subject towards being included as a citizen of the State, or does the political subject manage to change the imaginations of such a citizen subject? In other words, as the State grants one right to the political subject, what does it demand in return? Finally, as resistance dilutes in meaning, and there is a shift in signification, does it produce an excess that is unable to be co-opted within the discourse of rights and inclusive citizenship? If so, what happens to this excess?

In lieu of answers, Samaddar gives the example of women's movements in India, to say that in this quest for legal reform, what eludes the woman subject is justice in a Derridean sense (Derrida, 2002); to be the beneficiary of legal reform, the woman subject also has to be constructed as a citizen by a patriarchal State. While it is not that these patriarchal biases of the State have gone unnoticed by women's movements (Agnes, 2002; 2008), it is also true that "the law has become simultaneously the most used and criticized sphere for thinking about justice for women" (John, 2008, p. 266). In light of the dominance of the law in women's movements, as well as in queer politics in India, it is possible to argue that the political subjects of these movements have been drawn into the discourse of rights. However, it might be imperative to ask what is the cost of a right granted by the State and how the subject transforms in order to repay this cost.

This emphasis on law in queer politics in India is imbricated with discourses around inclusive and equal citizenship and human rights, which are demands made by queer subjects on the basis of experiences of marginalization because of sexual orientation and gender identity. These arguments are not limited to queer politics in India, however, and have been repeated so often in movements around queerness (and other 'minority' rights) in other parts of the world that the link between queer politics and identity politics has almost become naturalized, so much so that dominant ideas of queerness define it as an identity or orientation. Across transnational queer movements, sexuality is often articulated as an individual and personal choice or as something that is natural and inborn. The link between sexuality and naturalness is discursively produced through the help and support of science, the perpetual search for a 'gay gene' for example, where one hopes for social acceptance by the proxy effects of the power of science that validate homosexuality. While this discourse of non-heterosexuality as natural has been severely critiqued over time, from within queer politics and without, it can be argued that its insidious effects and affects still claim a hold on imaginations of sexuality and queerness (khanna, 2007; 2016).

But even as 'naturalness' begins to be problematized, gender and sexuality remain within the domain of personal choice, which frames the subject as an individual, as opposed to seeing subjectivity emerging out of collectivity, like Samaddar's imagination of the political subject. Once this discourse of sexuality as individual choice begins to take hold, there is a "consciousness of deprivation and a consequent necessity to assert 'rights'" (Bose & Bhattacharyya, 2007, p. xviii) around one's freedom to sexual choice and gender expression. The articulation of sexuality as choice and therefore its deprivation being taken as a matter of human rights is necessarily predicated on the role of such manifestations of sexuality and gender expression being seen as marginalized, and consequently in need of protection. This raises questions around the efficacy of the human rights paradigm in furthering queer politics, as well as the constructions of gender, sexuality, and the subject that accompany such an articulation.

Within this framework, human rights are required to do at least two things – first, to remind the public that those who had been hitherto classified as 'deviant' or 'abnormal' because of their sexuality or gender are human beings, and therefore deserve the same rights as everyone else; and, second, to seek justice for having been marginalized and for having gone through difficult and often traumatic experiences of pain, suffering, and otherness. There is an inherent paradox at work here – if human rights endeavour to equalize all individuals and bring them to a degree of sameness, then to seek human rights from a position that is situated in pain and suffering is predicated on being exceptional, which contradicts the very purpose of human rights as a tool towards achieving equality (Brown, 2004). At least two questions emerge here – first, about the grounding of human rights in experiences of marginalization and suffering; and, second, about the logic of the human rights framework and what it produces as politics and subjectivity.

If we agree that human rights essentialize experience, insofar they rely on experiences of marginalization and suffering in order to do justice to them, then we need to explore the processes behind such essentialization. For Scott (1992), to essentialize experience is to think of it as absolute truth, unmediated, pure, and outside the realm of questioning or critique. This is to discard the numerous ways in which meaning is made, and the inequalities in accessing the tools of meaning making that are grounded in language, history, economy, and other registers of privilege. The processes that make experience visible in this manner also make the inherent inequalities and privileges of signification and representation invisible, fixing identity and experience as reified categories and narratives. Extending this argument, if experience is naturalized, then it naturalizes the identity position from which this experience is articulated, and through this process, the truth of experience becomes an opaque and unquestionable field that hides its own constructions and positions, its own investments and divestments, and its own contradictions (Scott, 1992). In the case of queer narratives and the identity positions from which the claim to human rights is made, perhaps what is naturalized is the experience of suffering and pain. This also means that if the experience of (the suffering of) homosexuality is naturalized, it maintains heterosexuality because it comes to be signified in opposition to heterosexuality as inalienable and absolute difference. Homosexuality is a meaningful signifier of only that which is not heterosexuality, that which is therefore excluded from heterosexual privilege, and as such, perhaps it can be said to reinforce its own lack (through marginalization) in comparison to heterosexuality.

Further, the dangers of essentializing experience also lie in how easily it can disintegrate into what is perhaps unproductive relativism, where one experience is seen as untranslatable to another if it does not emerge from the same identity position. This maintains the legitimacy of all experience, while ensuring experience can no longer enter the productive field of collectivization, but remain – at best – as potential and contingent coalitions (Carastathis, 2013) that take place as political strategies that seem to ignore and obscure differences rather than engaging with them (Upadhyay & Ravecca, 2017). This, in turn, constructs the political subject as "fixed and autonomous" (Scott, 1992, p. 28), rather than engaging with identity as mutable and dynamic, which does not seem to allow for a properly productive political stance that can house the claim of being, for example, 'Queer and Dalit and Proud' (a placard carried during the Delhi Queer Pride Parade in 2015) or 'Indian and Lesbian' (a placard mounted during the protests against disruptions of screenings of *Fire* in 1998). Here, what does it mean to be queer *and* Dalit? How do caste and sexuality intersect in such an articulation? Or, what does it mean to be Indian *and* lesbian? While these enunciations and coalitions are possible, the naturalization of experience and ossification of identity categories makes these intersections seem like empty spaces of signification; it is not that they are devoid of meaning, for such expressions are indicative of something, but this 'something' is not fully signified, its meanings are as yet unclear. Perhaps this is because in such frameworks of thinking through experience, there is no space for simultaneously multiple articulations of identity. This logic also extends to take within its ambit the reification of the agency of a subject, while forgetting that agency is a result of the subject's situatedness in multiple and often contradictory social, cultural, economic, and political structures that have their own disciplinary logics of governmentality, and their own systems of productive power (Foucault, 1977).

However, naturalizing experience also holds the potential to be a reason for collectivization (but this would be a different collective as compared to one that does not have identity as its organizing principle), in the event of one identity position subsuming all others. This act of political unification comes with its own costs. According to Scott (1992), "The unifying aspect of experience excludes whole realms of human activity by simply not counting them as experience at least with any consequences for social organization or politics" (p. 30). As everyone gathers under the umbrella term 'queer', it renders irrelevant the differences of gender; as everyone gathers under the umbrella term 'woman', it renders irrelevant the differences of sexuality; as everyone gathers under the umbrella term 'transgender', it renders irrelevant the differences of body. In the process of differences being made redundant in order to unify (albeit temporarily), it is not that differences are transcended, or ignored; if narratives of members of LBT spaces are to be acknowledged, these differences are articulated within the coalition, and produce effects, affects, and marginalizations. Such unifications posit the individual as queer/woman/transgender first, and the subject of politics later. It is as if politics emerges out of experience, a linear process that creates an artificial temporality that cannot reverse itself; in other words, queerness is naturalized, and therefore not seen as produced through its own histories and politics. At the same time, it cannot be underscored enough that despite differences, coalitions do come together, and manage to have a somewhat fruitful relation, however tenuous, even if in the direction towards human rights.

To be clear, to question the reliance on experience is not to question the narrative of suffering that queer lives have tended to present to us. Any engagement with either queer politics or queer theory will demonstrate the unending productions of violence onto the queer body and psyche, and the nefarious and multiple ways in which heterosexuality asserts its dominance explicitly and implicitly on queer lives (see Chapter 4). Perhaps it might be important to locate the reasons behind this insistence, this repetition – why do queer narratives always demonstrate violence? What is it in the organization of the socio-cultural systems that surround queer lives that produces the material effects of violence so easily? What is being elaborated here is not a question on the content of experience, but on the process of that experience presenting itself as evidence, particularly in relation to the human rights framework. If we agree that human rights naturalize experience, and experience naturalizes identities, then we cannot but enter into the question of the effects of the human rights framework. What do human rights achieve, and as such, where do they lead the subject of queer identity politics?

The demand of human rights and the desire for inclusion

Insofar as queer politics in India, and elsewhere, seems inextricably tied to the discourse of human rights, we must wonder what kinds of subjectivities this discourse produces; specifically, what the effects and affects of human rights are in determining queer subjects and queer politics. For Brown (2004):

> human rights are vague and unenforceable; their content is infinitely malleable; they are more symbolic than substantive; they cannot be grounded in any ontological truth or philosophical principle; in their primordial individualism; they conflict with cultural integrity and are a form of liberal imperialism; they are a guise in which superpower domination drapes itself; they are a guise in which globalization of capital drapes itself; they entail secular idolatry of the human and are thus as much a religious creed as any other.
>
> *(p. 451)*

Brown later goes on to elaborate how, in the name of reducing suffering and striving towards inclusion, human rights protect "individuals who may trade one form of subjection for another, [providing] an intervention by an external agent or set of institutions that promises to protect individuals from abusive state power in part by replacing that power" (Ibid., p. 455). If we return to Samaddar's (2010) understanding of the political subject, not only do human rights irrevocably frame the subject as individual and apolitical, thereby negating any possibility of a collective emergence of the political subject; they also erase the differentiated ways in which subjects are positioned that determine their ability to enter human rights discourse. Perhaps there is a cost of being included, and insofar as queer politics is linked with the human rights framework, it becomes imperative to ask what these costs are, and whether all queer subjects pay them equally.

Critique emerging in parts of the world where queer politics has already fallen prey to homonormative tendencies (Duggan, 2003) reveals clear fulfillments of homonationalist moments (Puar, 2017), and the assimilation of middle- or upper-class, able bodied, mostly White queer subjects into the logic of nationhood, neoliberalism, and capitalism demonstrates how such projects of inclusion are built at the cost of excluding queer subjects who are poor, disabled, and people of colour (Gross, 2017; Haritaworn, 2017; Upadhyay & Ravecca, 2017). According to Haritaworn, Kuntsman, and Posocco (2013), these inclusions can quite literally be murderous by shifting the focus from their violence to their promise. For them, "[q]ueer citizenship, here, is conceptualized as a deadly mechanism of differentiated inclusion, which divides its subjects into grievable and ungrievable, worthy and unworthy of state protection, 'folded into life' or 'socially dead'" (p. 446). If inclusion is indeed murderous, it is not so only in its real and systemic murders of queer lives outside the structure (that might manifest as suicides), but also in the differentiated margins it creates within queer subjects who must now contend not only with violence from outside – the violence of the norm(al) – but also focus on the violence they exhibit on each other. Within the new stratifications of queerness, there are layers of what is acceptable, appropriated, and entirely outsided, and these stratifications are what make emergent solidarities and collectivities difficult.

In such frameworks of disaggregated margins (Chen, 2012), or margins of margins (Chaudhury, Das, & Chakrabarti, 2000), there are surrogate centres of power that create a topology of subjects divided into concentric circles; the closer subjects are to the centres of power, the more included they are within its structure. Similar to Rubin's formulation of the 'charmed circle' (2011), in this theorization of subjects as they are formed in relation to power, some are positioned at the boundaries of centres of power, and some are absolutely outsided. Given this framework, and given that there are surrogate centres of power in the field of queer politics, who are the absolutely outsided subjects of the framework of queer politics? What do the subjects of queer politics who demand inclusion do to create those outsided subjects? Further, what does it mean for a queer subject to be included?

Graham and Slee (2006) posit that there is a difference between the act of inclusion and being inclusive. This distinction is made possible by asking the question – what is one seeking to be included in? Inevitably, it is structure; the term 'inclusion' "presupposes a whole into which something (or someone) can be incorporated. It would be reasonable to argue that there is an implicit centred-ness to the term *inclusion*" (p. 4). Such an idea of inclusion conceives of a clear demarcation of the inside and outside of a structure; there is a sense of fixed boundaries that goes against notions of porosity, nomadicity, and migration in such frameworks. It follows then, that inclusion would maintain the centrality of the structure, thereby leaving the 'structurality of the structure' (Derrida, 1967/1978) untouched. Here, if the demand is that the nation needs to include the 'queer', then what we perhaps need to address is the heterosexual and patriarchal logic of the nation (Pateman, 1988; 1889), which models a corresponding citizen for whom reproductive heterosexuality is the norm (Spivak, 2005), and then wonder what the inclusion of the homosexual or the transgender subject into such a structure might achieve. For, according to Derrida (1967/1978): "the organizing principle of the structure would limit what we might call the play of the structure . . . At the center, the permutation or transformation of elements (which may of course be structures enclosed within a structure) is forbidden" (p. 352).

To engage with the inclusion of the queer subject into the folds of the nation would require an acknowledgement that inclusion would allow the queer subject some contingent freedoms, basic nominal rights, and as such, would be an efficient tool in reducing their experiences of marginalization and othering (Anthias, 2013). We cannot simply deny the role of identity based human rights in alleviating the suffering of those who had hitherto lived without some basic access to dignity. As queer persons, it is difficult to access education, employment, and housing; public spaces often become warzones, and there is immense bias from institutions that are promised to all citizens, such as healthcare, legal aid, and others, not to mention the socio-cultural pressures felt by virtue of being queer.

However, to understand the demand to include the queer subject as a subject of rights and identity would also raise some questions. We could ask whether those who demand inclusion have fully acknowledged what it would mean to be included. For example, would they know the implications of being 'Indian and Lesbian'? While I concede that the placard was contingently necessary, since the time in which it was raised and made popular was a time when the lesbian figure in India was almost entirely invisible, I would still like to examine what might lie beneath the need to claim an 'Indian-ness' alongside one's lesbian identity. What policies of the Indian State would the Indian lesbian endorse and support, for example? What would it mean to be included and accepted as 'Indian and Lesbian' in other words? This leads to questions that can be asked about the transformative potential of such politics, and also about the process of inclusion itself. Not only would we ask what *is* the subject being included into, but we could also ask, what *of* the subject is being included? What of the subject is being incorporated inside the structure, and what of the subject is being left outside? If the central logic of the structure cannot be transformed, and if that logic is indeed that of reproductive heterosexuality, then how is the queer subject being included? Further, if the logic of reproductive heteronormativity cannot be open to any mutation in such a process of inclusion, then how is it that the queer political subject is being transmuted via inclusion?

In the entire process of inclusion, there is the implicit assumption that the centre of the structure holds a norm (Graham & Slee, 2006), and that norm – while sustaining the structure – lies outside the structure (Derrida, 1967/1978). In other words, because the norm is the structuring principle, it is itself removed from the structure. We could perhaps say that this norm is imbued with materiality, for it produces what seems like the truth of the 'normal' subject, while also holding onto its abstracted properties which allow for it to transcend materiality. The subject who is outsided by this norm would have to contend with the demands of its material truth on the subject, as well as its abstract and a priori sense of power. In addition, to be inside (the logic of) the structure is to reinforce the invisibility of its centrality, it is to maintain its norm, but implicitly. While the queer subject is outsided by the norm of reproductive heterosexuality, it feels its material effects and affects, even embodies this outsided-ness; it can see the norm for the material effects it produces, including the affects of trauma, pain, and suffering, corresponding here with a fundamental positioning as the Other of heterosexuality. At the same time, the queer subject, however outsided, can still be governed by reproductive heterosexuality, for the norm has its hold on subjects inside its fold, as well as subjects outside it, albeit differently.

Therefore, as the subject of queer politics begins to become included, perhaps it can be said that the subject is being taken into the fold of reproductive heterosexuality. This is rather contrary, and returns us to the question of whether the subject is being incorporated into reproductive heterosexuality at the cost of its radical queerness. According to Graham and Slee (2006), inclusion that does not shift the logic of the structure, nor its governing principle, and consequently its boundaries, is inclusion that creates the illusion of interiority while parts of the subject are exteriorized, placed outside, made Other, such that what is excluded cannot even be articulated in a discourse and language of the inside that the subject must now adopt. And so, we can ask: if the Rights of Transgender Persons Bill of 2014 aims to include the transgender figure into the nation, does it do so at the cost of excluding that of the transgender that could question the stability of reproductive heterosexuality? Does it incorporate the difference between binary gender and transgender simply by claiming that the transgender figure comprises of a minority aberration of what is the normalcy of gender, and therefore must be given extra benefits in order to make up for their lack? Once the transgender figure comes within this ambit of inclusion through legal process, do they have to reassert their underprivileged positions? Do they have to embody their abnormal difference without threatening the norm of the normal?

In such a framework of inclusion without being inclusive, it is not that the violent process of exteriorization and creation of the Other is transcended in any real way; it is simply that those who have entered the fold of inclusion are no longer at the margins outside (even if they are at the margins inside), and are replaced by other subjects who become Other, who feel the traumatic effects of being excluded. Since the logic of the structure remains the same, its processes do not change – it is only subjects who are taken in, parts of them expelled, to create other Others, still outside. There is a displacement of positions; borders are crossed and newer subjects produced even as the structure and its effects remain, and all the while subjects for whom crossing borders is impossible linger on. What changes is that now subjects who were previously outside and have recently been subjected to (and subjectivated by) inclusion become complicit in reproducing the violence of the norm(al). The problem with this framework of inclusion is that it misrepresents the included queer subject, the norm effaces its queerness, the subject is substituted as a result of being included. This is the cost of inclusion.

If the cost of inclusion is so high, why is inclusion so important to the subject of queer politics? Within a frame of disaggregation, where the queer subject is at the margins of being inside and outside, occupying multiple and contradictory positions simultaneously, what happens to their politics, and what happens to an understanding of queer political field? Is there something behind, or under, the insistence for inclusion? Is there something driving the queer subject towards law, revolving within its discourse? Where does the desire (for resistance) lie if the queer subject reiterates its demand for human rights?

II. The queer subject of psychoanalysis

To say that the queer political subject makes demands and adopts strategies based on identity politics to reap the benefits of inclusion into normative structures is an important indicator of the directions in which queer politics is heading (particularly in India, where homonationalism has not been actualized, but nationalist tendencies are on the rise), but perhaps is not enough to explain the queer political subject in its multifacetedness. A theorization of politics where the subject is constructed through mechanisms of power – power that objectifies the subject from outside, divides the subject from within, and helps a subject recognize herself as a subject (Foucault, 1980) – can help demonstrate the instrumentality and generativity of power on the subject, but perhaps cannot account for how the subject will transcend that power in a way that cannot again be co-opted by its logic (Copjec, 1994). In fact, critique of queer politics in India and the rest of the world is mounted on this very impulse of queer subjects to practise a politics of identity and inclusion – something that brings some queer subjects closer to centres of power – that allows for the radical potential of queerness to be co-opted by violently neoliberal and capitalist projects. The political, theoretical, and psychic shift required to imagine a subject whose resistance cannot be co-opted require us to think through relations of power. These relations of power then help construct micro-histories that help illustrate the numerous ways in which the subject subjects itself to power relations, while also creating many borderzones and several modes of production of power that locate the subject in shifting positions as opposed to in an absolute situatedness. This is the process of subjectivation, which Butler (1997) describes as denoting "both the becoming of the subject and the process of subjection" (p. 83).

This can help us see why and how the queer political subject might be implicated in not only their own subjection, but also in erasing the narratives of other subjects, queer or otherwise. Such an understanding of the subject in relation to power can explain how certain queer subjects, because of their gender, class, caste, race, or cultural capital of another kind, find themselves *speaking for* other queer subjects who do not have access to cultural, social, or economic capital, instead of *speaking with* them. Within a structure of disaggregated margins, such analysis can help reveal the motivations of a subject that strives for inclusion into dominant models, often choosing power over solidarity. If law is seen as the legitimizing principle of power (Derrida, 2002), it is possible to imagine a queer subject and queer politics striving to be on the side of legitimacy, and therefore, power, insofar as they are entangled in politics that is oriented towards legal reform.

In this framework of power relations, the queer political subject can be said to be responsible for maintaining unequal relations and economies of power with respect to other queer subjects. As I have tried to map through the previous chapters, fissures along the lines of gender (between male queer subjects and female queer subjects), sexuality (between heterosexual women subjects and queer women subjects), economy (between those who work on HIV/AIDS and those who do not), and culture (between the transgender, transsexual, hijra, and kothi subjects) create contestations of power within the queer community, and while these inequalities do not end coalitions between sections of queer subjects (for the most part), they impact the nature of queer politics in India and make solidarities difficult. As such, it is perhaps possible to say that the queer political subject who authors such politics also produces subjects of queer politics, subjected to the effects of such politics, but who are not in a position to author it in turn. This is where the entry of the subaltern position is possible in relation to the queer subject, mapped onto the scene of queer politics as envisioned in this work (see Chapter 5).

However, what such a model of power relations can perhaps not explain is how any imaginations of resistance will be operationalized within such a frame, especially if we see resistance as that phenomenon in politics – and that characteristic of the political subject – that will oppose power with desire (Samaddar, 2010). This model perhaps does not account for why the subject remains in their subjected location, why a form of resistance that cannot be coopted by power is barred for this subject. Within its logic, there does not seem to be any form of resistance that cannot be appropriated once again by the structures of power it is trying to oppose in the first place (Copjec, 1994); this is perhaps the case with the demand for human rights and inclusion by queer politics, where what was once radical and imagined as resistance now runs the risk of appropriation. In other words, this framework does not account for desire (Copjec, 1994), does not take seriously the question of the psyche of the subject in her own subjectivation (Butler, 1997). It posits power as transcendental, and as such, power has no limits. This is where the problem seems to be located.

To shift attention to desire from power, to the psyche as "the limits of normalization" (Butler, 1997, p. 88), then, might be an important and necessary step to take. It would throw up some questions, including but not limited to – what is the desire behind inclusion in queer politics? What can we learn from the demand for human rights made by the queer political subject? What is the relation of demand to desire? What does it tell us about the queer political subject? How does a turn to desire impact the queerness of the political subject, and how does it *queer* politics? What does a turn to the psyche – and therefore, psychoanalysis – do to understandings of the queer political subject?

Between subjectivation and subjectivization

For Butler (1997), Foucault's notion of subjectivation is one where the subject is actively produced by power through the material and physical effects power has on the subject. As such, the normalization of the subject is one that is enacted on the body, as well as what Foucault terms 'soul', which Butler interprets as "a kind of psychic identity" (p. 85). Here, the combined normalization of body and soul create a totalitarian sense of identity, which creates a coherent subject. But, for Butler, the notion of the subject is decentred by the psyche. The psyche exceeds the normalizing demands to be a coherent subject or inhabit a singular identity. She asks, "if Foucault understands the psyche to be an imprisoning effect in the service of normalization, then how might he account for psychic resistance to normalization?" (Ibid., p. 87). While there might be a problem of translation in a formulation where 'psyche' is used in place of 'soul', Butler's point remains crucial; in inaugurating the psyche somewhere akin to what Foucault called soul, Butler is opening up the Foucauldian subject to interiority that does not allow for a coherent, cogent subject. Just as Foucault demonstrates how power is productive, generative, structural, and negative, Butler demonstrates how the psyche can have power over the (Foucauldian) subject.

The entry of the psyche into theorizations of subjectivity introduces figurations of the unconscious in relation to formations of the subject, and if a framework of Lacanian psychoanalysis is being followed, like here, then it introduces the subject as one who is caught in language. He states, "it is the whole *structure of language* that psychoanalytic experience discovers in the unconscious ... language, with its structure, exists prior to each subject's entry into it" (Lacan, 1957/2006, p. 413. Emphasis mine). What Lacan is explicitly demarcating between is the structure of language and speech, where speech is what the subject utters, but (the structure of) language is what determines the structure of the unconscious, thereby determining the subject and their speech. Here, the subject enters into language, where language pre-dates the subject, such that the unconscious is now structured like a language. The provisional divide that is being made between language and speech is between the unconscious subject and the conscious speaking subject. However, it is not that the conscious and unconscious are opposite to each other. The unconscious is an active and dynamic process, and is determined by the push and pull of psychic mechanisms, the condensation and displacement of desire (Zupancic, 2016). The conscious subject is not only influenced by the unconscious, but also influences unconscious workings simultaneously. This interdependence also ensures that the subject is perpetually caught in a dialectic between the two.

The imaginary subject, or the conscious subject, for Lacan, is the subject of the ego ideal, which is entirely distinct from the subject of the unconscious, in that what we see of the subject in the conscious imaginary is not the subject at all; the subject is *elsewhere*. The ego ideal, represented as '*a*' in Lacanian psychoanalysis, is the place from where the subject articulates as 'I'. It is what enables the subject to speak of themselves, and embrace identity positions. However, this notion of the ego ideal, or 'I', is inherently based on alienation that stems from a process of misrecognition (or méconnaissance) in the subject. In what Lacan calls the 'mirror stage' (1949/2006):

> imaginary identification occurs in the subject through the unconscious assumption of an external image (initially of the subject's own body as reflected in a mirror) in which he recognizes himself. . . . the ego can first be created only because the image irremediably "traps" the subject.
>
> *(Chiesa, 2007, p. 15)*

There are at least two things of note here. First, to identify oneself in a mirror image is an act based on double misrecognition since one cannot ever see their whole body at one time, and further, the mirror image is the inverse of oneself. Second, the ego ideal emerges in this process of misrecognition, and insofar as it establishes "a relationship between an organism and its reality" (Lacan, 1949/2006, p. 78), that reality is necessarily based on misrecognition.

In such a theorization of the ego ideal, or I function, the ego ideal has an agential role in the process of misrecognition, but not only does it lead to a subject whose reality is skewed, literally as if the subject is seeing the inverse and accepting it as real, but it also creates a subject that has forgotten its fragmentation since it has somehow seen itself as whole in the mirror, an act of visualization that is physically impossible. As Chiesa (2007) writes:

> Imaginary identification can consequently be said to be alienating by definition; in addition to this, the alienated ego also fails to recognize its own functioning. Thus, a double misrecognition (méconnaissance) takes place: in fact, the ego not only, as it were, "finds itself" at the place of the other (the first misrecognition: the ego is alienated) but also provides the subject with a deceptive impression of unity (the second and most fundamental misrecognition: the ego does not recognize itself as alienated).
>
> *(p. 16)*

The I function of the conscious subject, therefore, is one that pretends to posit the subject as whole, when the subject is actually a fragmented, decentred subject. Torn between conscious and unconscious, both having their own divergent and tendentious logics, any portrayal of the subject as a singular subject is problematic, or based on forgetting and misrecognition of subjecthood.

About the mirror stage Lacan writes: "the ego is only completed by being articulated not as the *I* of discourse, but as a metonymy of its signification" (1960/2006, p. 685). Here, the linguistic function of metonymy is synonymous with the psychic function of displacement, and Lacan seems to be saying that the ego ideal is not only a cause of alienation for the subject, but is also unable to locate the subject; the subject is displaced. This is because the subject, for Lacan, is a subject only because it has entered language, encountered the symbolic, and is thereby determined by the unconscious. The ego, relegated to the imaginary register, is unable to account for such a subject. What this demonstrates to us is that the subject who articulates from the I position is not fully capable of articulating its position. Also, as the unconscious influences the imaginary, the subject speaks something other than what it intends to say; unconscious speech is speaking through the imaginary subject by subverting its autonomous agency. This is not to say that the conscious subject has no agency whatsoever, and is only governed by the unconscious. According to Lacan (1949/2006):

> this form situates the agency known as the ego, prior to its social determination, in a fictional direction that will forever remain

irreducible for any single individual or, rather, that will only asymptotically approach the subject's becoming, no matter how successful the dialectical synthesis by which he must resolve, as *I*, his discordance with his own reality.

(p. 76)

Here, the function of agency is to distract the subject and maintain its discordance with reality, as well as its alienation, and the character of such agency is fictive, in that it does not truly locate the subject in its path, but constantly places it elsewhere, misplaces the subject from itself.

Another feature of the mirror stage is the introduction of the *other* for the subject. As the subject first recognizes itself in the mirror, surpassing its own fragmentation and thereby entering alienation, the subject who is then an infant also becomes related to the other who is holding her up to the mirror. The human propping her up is incorporated as other, and as such it is a sign of how the ego ideal of the subject is always dependent on the other while being directed towards the other. In this process of incorporation, the other's ego (represented as a') becomes a part of the subject, such that it eventually comes to represent a split within the Lacanian subject. This other is the incorporated imaginary other, bearing semblance with parts of the self, giving the appearance of reality. The imaginary dialectic between the ego ideal a and the other a' marks one trajectory of the subject; this pathway is influenced by the larger scheme of the symbolic, in relation to which this pathway demonstrates its purpose. The imaginary register serves as a distraction from the processes of the symbolic while being determined by them nonetheless, such that speech reveals and hides at the same time, like the psychoanalytic symptom.

Such a decentration of the subject into the subject of the unconscious and conscious speaking subject (with competing logics, motives, drives, and desires) has implications for an understanding of the agential, identitarian subject of queer politics. If we tried to bring these two understandings of the subject together, we would perhaps not be able to escape the problem of identity with respect to the queer political subject. According to Cuellar (2010), within the Lacanian frame, if we believe that there is similarity based on identity, then we forget to respect difference. On the imaginary register, words or signs imply similarities, since one sign is assumed to refer to one meaning only. For example, here, like in Saussure's linguistics, the sign 'lesbian' would indicate only one signified, one meaning. Within this frame, all lesbian women could come together based on their identity – similarity (in meaning) would transcend difference (of class, caste, geography, etc.). While Foucauldian theory reminds us that there are multiple vectors of power, and as such, solidarity on the basis of one identity could only be temporary and reproductive of power relations itself, Lacanian theory would perhaps take another route and say the imaginary register, unrepresentative as it is of the subject itself, could never author lasting political alliances. If the subject is truly decentred, caught in the dialectic between conscious and unconscious agency, then perhaps it is the essentialization of experience that can come into question as well. If the unconscious produces the desires and drives of the subject, then they cannot claim full ownership or authorship of the representation of their experience since they cannot fully access that which is the determining effect or affect of unconscious processes. As such, the symbolic subject of the unconscious must be breached in order to reach another understanding of the queer political subject, one that accounts for the psyche as well as the political.

In Lacanian theory, the subject of the unconscious corresponds to the register of the symbolic (without being synonymous with it), where the unconscious is structured like a language, and the smallest unit of language – the signifier – becomes vital in understanding the subject's relationship to language. Here, language has its own structure, its own grammatical rules, and the subject who is introduced in language must now grapple with the effects of being caught, like a fish in a hook, within its logic. This seemingly inevitable entrapment is due to "culture . . . which may well be reduced to language, that is, to what essentially distinguishes human society from natural societies" (Lacan, 1957/2006, p. 414). This is, perhaps, the heart of Lacanian matter. Language is what introduces the subject into culture, makes the subject human. Language, in Lacanian theory, is related to the (formation of the) subject where the:

> human subject [is] *split* by her use of language . . . determined by language. The subject as so determined is fixed, tied down, or pinned down in the process . . . the subject becomes *fixated* here, or subjected to something else. It is a limiting, delimiting process.
> *(Fink, 2004, p. 115)*

And language is what inaugurates the Other, thereby birthing desire, and instituting the Law, where all three concepts are linked to each other, and make up the stuff of the symbolic order.

According to Chiesa (2007), the "Other may be equated with: (a) *language* as a structure (as in structural linguistics); (b) *the symbolic order* as the legal fabric of human culture (in accordance with Levi-Strauss's anthropology); (c) *the Freudian unconscious* as reformulated by Lacan" (p. 35). As the subject becomes linked to the Other, they become a subject in language, of the symbolic, with unconscious agency that is apposite to the agency of consciousness. The Other is the figure in the Lacanian symbolic that the subject of the unconscious is addressing through language. As such, the Other emerges alongside the subject's entry into language. Lacan writes:

> The Other, as preliminary site of the pure subject of the signifier, occupies the key position [in the subject's graph of desire, or the graph of subjectivity] . . . one cannot even speak of a code without it already being the Other's code; something quite different is at stake in the message, since the subject constitutes himself on the basis of this message, such that he receives from the Other even the message he himself sends [albeit in an inverted form].
> *(1960/2006, p. 683)*

This is to reiterate that the speech of the subject is directed perpetually towards the Other, and inasmuch as it is determined by that direction, it conveys more – and something else – than what the subject consciously intends. If such is the queer political subject, perhaps it might be helpful to think about the Other of queer politics, towards whom/which speech is directed and the demand is made, for the Lacanian subject directs its demand to the Other, having been caught in a traction-like circuit of desire with the Other, such that "[d]esire is desire for desire, the Other's desire, as I have said, in other words, subjected to the Law" (Lacan, 1964/2006, p. 723). This will also raise the question of what the queer political subject desires – or, *what is the queer political subject's circuit of desire?*

A simple understanding of the Lacanian subject might be that as the subject enters language (is hooked by language), pre-verbal need gets converted into demand, and the remainder of that conversion (which can be akin to a process of division) is desire. The circuit of desire establishes the dialectic between the subject and its Other, but this very dialectic ensures that the subject and its Other never meet. Desire remains alive in the distance between the subject and its Other, and the function of desire is to keep the subject in a position of a symbolic lack that maintains desire. In the circuit by which the subject makes a demand of the Other, the Other can only reciprocate in part (partly to keep desire alive, and partly because the Other is precisely that which cannot reciprocate in full). This part is the *objet a*, the part object given back by the Other that now becomes the centre of the circuit of desire. Desire, in Lacan, also simultaneously inaugurates the Law, such that desire and the Law emerge together. The Law here refers to the fundamental prohibition on originary desire – for the maternal principle – where "[t]he law forbidding incest is the locus of this economy of kinship that forbids endogamy" (Butler, 1990, p. 42). This is the foundational Law that turns the subject outwards, the price to be paid for induction into culture, the hook of language. For Lacan, Law can be read as that which governs the subject as soon as it enters language. It is the principle that governs desire in order for discontent to be the condition of civilization. The idea of the Law can also be read with respect to gender and sexuality, where it helps place the subject in an 'ideal sex' (Lacan, 1958/2006, p. 575) and ensures thereon that its effects are heterosexual. One such reading of the Law led Butler (1990) to describe the formation of gender as melancholy, and the Law as dividing the subject into two genders that were opposed to each other in a way that maintained the stasis of heterosexuality. Since desire here arises alongside its prohibition, the subject of the unconscious is fundamentally barred from its desire, represented as $\bar{S}$. I hypothesize that the bar between Signifier and Signified in the Lacanian schema is the bar on the symbolic subject, where Signifier/Signified leads to $\bar{S}$, or the barred subject. This is because desire is prohibited only as the subject is introduced into language, and therefore, culture. The prohibitive principle that maintains culture, and bars the subject of the unconscious from its desire, is the same bar of (the unit of) language. And so, the subject in the Lacanian schema is subjectivized; between demand and desire, between the imaginary and the symbolic, between self and Other.

This formulation of the subject raises questions for the queer political subject. If it is true that resistance is a matter of desire (Samaddar, 2010), then it has to deal with the decentred $\bar{S}$ of the unconscious. Since this subject is caught on the tenterhooks of language and a logical agency of the unconscious that counters the agency of the conscious singular subject, it is the dialectic that might be seen as productive of understanding the nature of queer politics, and as such, the queer political subject. Perhaps the questions that emerge here are: where does political resistance lie – in the imaginary, or in the symbolic, and what is the nature of this resistance? What is the role of psychic processes in resisting power, and, what is the role of psychic processes in resisting the resistance of power?

Between political resistance and psychoanalytic resistance

The Lacanian subject is characterized by an intersubjective relationship between the subject and its Other that is dialectic in nature. Perhaps it can be claimed that the Lacanian subject is perpetually a subject that remains placed between two tendentious pulls. It is this intersubjectivity that grounds the subject in culture (consciously and unconsciously, in the imaginary and the symbolic), which exteriorizes the unconscious process and reveals the role of the structure of language and culture in its symbolic effects/affects. This, in turn, shifts the clear boundaries of what is interior to the subject and what is exterior for the subject, and this interiority and exteriority also produces another dialectic for the Lacanian subject. What is shown below is what Lacan (1966/2006) termed the L Schema, an image to demonstrate the role of intersubjectivity in the subject, between the (shy of the) subject and the (beyond of the) Other:

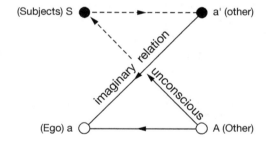

FIGURE 3.1 The L Schema, Lacan (1966/2006)

Here, the barred subject (S) oscillates between the imaginary register, where the two poles are that of the ego ideal a and the imaginary incorporated other a', and the symbolic register of the unconscious, where the two poles are that of the subject of the unconscious, S, and the symbolic Other, or A.

The Lacanian subject maintains an ambivalent relationship between the two registers, see-sawing between one and the other (Other), influenced by both. Desire is born between the subject (S) and the Other (A). The four positions on the schema show how the subject (S) and the Other

(A) are linked and how the ego ideal (a) and the incorporated other (a') are tied together, but also displays how the Other (A) has an impact on the ego ideal (a), as well as the role of the subject (S) on the incorporated other (a'). Here, the placement reveals to us that the Other (A) impacts the ego ideal (a) without the conscious subject being fully cognizant of it. Perhaps what the relation between the subject of the unconscious (S) and the other (a') hints at is the way in which the subject (S) determines the incorporation of the other (a').

I hypothesize that this schema is important in understanding the queer political subject who is also the decentred subject of psychoanalysis at the same time. The role of the unconscious not only problematizes the singular similarities of identity positions and the linearity of essentialized experiences, but is crucial in understanding what lies hidden behind the demand for human rights, and what it might mean for queer politics to desire inclusion. The object of desire – *objet a* – hidden from the queer political subject but determining the circuit of desire that the queer political subject is destined to follow might be helpful in understanding the nature of this subject and their relationship with queer politics. It might also help reveal the role of psychoanalytic resistance to politics (what of queer subjects who are not involved in queer politics, or what of queer political subjects who may not have a *queer* outlook towards the queer political field), while also elucidating their presence or absence of political resistance in queer politics. As such, the L Schema can now be redrawn as below:

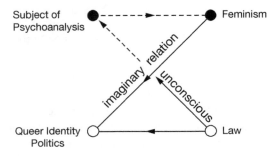

FIGURE 3.2 Reimagining the L Schema for the queer/political/subject

Here, the subject of psychoanalysis has come to take the position of the subject (S), feminism has come to take the position of the incorporated other (a'), Law has occupied the position of the Other (A), and queer identity has replaced the ego ideal (*a*) from its position. The imaginary register and symbolic register remain the same, such that at the two poles of the imaginary lie the misrecognized ego ideal of queer identity and the incorporated other of feminism, and at the two poles of the symbolic lie the decentred subject of psychoanalysis and Law as the Other. Between these intersubjective dialectics lies the (fate of the) subject who authors queer politics, barred from its desire.

The implications of redrawing the L schema to fit the field of queer politics and locate the shifting queer political subject can be various. In placing the subject of psychoanalysis at the position of the symbolic subject of the unconscious is to try and think through a queer political subject who is decentred, with unconscious drives, and circuits of desire that are unknown, whose speech is an echo of what it addresses to its Other. It is to also try and rethink the very nature of queer politics – will it now be a field that is less certain of itself, its directions, its drives, and its utopias? Will we be able to think of queer politics that can claim to not fully know its determinations, and as such reflects on its present coalitions as signs and symptoms of its desire, beyond the trope of political strategy and necessity? To place psychoanalysis in the position of the subject of the unconscious is not to make psychoanalysis the subject, or even analyse the subject, but to render the hitherto political subject psychoanalytic.

The position of feminism in the place of the other (*a'*) can be fitting, insofar as queer politics (at least as imagined by LBT collectives and groups) sees feminism as its natural ally and the women's movement as its most important comrade. Feminism then, becomes that which is incorporated by queer politics and its subject, albeit in the register of the imaginary. This position of feminism as within the imaginary seems important, insofar as it hints at being unable to reach the subject of the unconscious, and this raises some questions.[1] If feminism, like the politics of queer identity (positioned here in place of the ego ideal *a*), remains in the register of the imaginary, how does it account for the psychoanalytic subject? And, further, how does it account for psychoanalytic resistance in the subject of its politics? What happens to the queer political subject who battles with internalized homophobia, or who refuses to recognize their own patriarchal privilege? What of the woman who refuses to leave her marriage despite continuous domestic abuse? How is a feminist queer politics of the imaginary equipped to handle such a subject? Perhaps the answer lies in relation to psychoanalysis; in the reformulated L Schema, it is psychoanalysis (in place of the Subject of the unconscious) that acts upon feminism, and through that, on the politics of queer identity.

Perhaps psychoanalysis is where we will discover the reason behind subjectivization, and the decentred subject will help us think through our centered politics, as well as the centres of our politics.

As I have tried to demonstrate, the role of law is vital for queer politics, just as it was crucial for the women's movement. In an earlier section of this chapter, what surfaced, perhaps rather potently, was the divide between the legality and the symbolic value of Section 377. It was argued that the presence of Section 377 in the Indian Penal Code is restrictive towards any imagination of a queer Indian citizen subject (Narrain & Bhan, 2005; Narrain, 2007a; 2007b). To place Law in the position of the Other (*A*) in the reformulated L Schema is to highlight this symbolic function of the Law. It can be argued that queer politics remains somewhat trapped in the subversion of legal practices that are a result of Section 377, which can be said to be on the imaginary register, while the real power of Section 377 comes from its symbolic hold on the imaginary; it *literally* blocks the Indian nation-state from formulating any conception of a non-heterosexual non-binary gendered citizen subject. Perhaps one could say that by remaining within the discourse of Law at the imaginary register, the queer political subject plays into the desire of the nation-state, a desire to include the citizen without including their queerness, to incorporate the queer political subject in the discourse of the nation-state.

If Law, at the level of the symbolic, is the Other of the queer political subject, then what is the *objet a* returned by the Other around which this subject will build its circuit of desire? This is the hidden desire of the queer political subject, revealed not even to itself, even as they operate as a subject who *knows* this desire, and revolve around it. Is this desire that of inclusion? Is it the desire to be the same as the heterosexual subject? Is this desire one that straightens the queer path of the queer political subject into one that is most trodden? For we cannot forget the cost of queerness, the real subject effects that sexuality produces in queer subjects that are often alienating, frequently painful, repeatedly traumatic. Is this the dialectic within which the queer political subject remains, oscillating between the pressure to be radical and the burden to be heterosexual? Between normality and abnormality, what does the queer political subject resist – what does the queer political subject resist politically, what does it resist psychoanalytically, and what is the relation between the two? For Lacan, the subject always knows the truth, and "the question for psychoanalysis is *how to tie the regimes of knowledge and truth together*" (Fink, 2004, p. 110). The subject knows its desire, but is not aware of it. And so, what does the queer political subject do about its desire to be included, and the cost at which desire is maintained, never to be fulfilled? If inclusion is at the heart of desire, then where does the desire for resistance lie? What happens to the desire for political resistance, for a radical subversion of the reproductive heteronorm?

While Samaddar accounts for a particular kind of political subject, whose resistance – insofar as it is not amenable to being co-opted by power – is on the side of desire, he does not explicitly state that desire is what opens this subject up to (Lacanian) psychoanalysis. I would like to contend that while our usual understandings of political resistance operate on the imaginary register, psychoanalytic resistance is seen in the symbolic register; it is this slippage between the two kinds of resistances that account for the subject's position in the middle of their dialectic. This dialectic, while making political subjects of us, does not necessarily ensure that our psyches are also included within many contemporary theorizations of politics. If we see the hold of the social and cultural (especially through the potency of Law) on the psyche and think of it as producing psychoanalytic resistances that fix a subject in its subjectivated place, then we can also see how a politics in the imaginary may not necessarily reach the Subject. This might be manifested in a divide between what is personal and what becomes political. And so, we can ask, if the task of politics is to revolutionize not only society, but also subjectivity, can a politics that does not account for the psyche succeed?

Perhaps the difference between the registers of political and psychoanalytic resistance can also be seen as the root of untranslatability in political moments that irrupt, in languages that are not fully articulable, not understood by those who are its interlocutors. Perhaps such moments can be found in the protest by Mothers of Manorama in Manipur, where women protested naked outside the Indian Army Headquarters against the rape and murder of Thangjam Manorama Devi. As these women urged the army to rape them, their protest was seen by many as shocking and unique, in turn revealing the extraordinary conditions of lives under the Armed Forces Special Powers Act (AFSPA) (Chakravarti, 2010). The nakedness of these women's bodies produced a kind of symbolic meaning whose logic could not be co-opted by a politics of, or in support of, the Indian nation-state. Another example can be seen by deconstructing the 'I Am 43' movement in Mexico, which took place in response to the kidnapping of a group of 43 students on their way to commemorate a government massacre. Their friends, families, and supporters refused to grieve their deaths, and demanded that the 43 students be returned to them. In this case, the refusal to mourn produced a language of incommensurability, and the government was faced with a demand they could not meet. In both protests, there is no room for negotiation with the State, and nothing can be returned by the State to the protesters – it may be that for those who were protesting, the State was truly Other and produced an irreducible untranslatability that preserved the impossible relation.

It is through such moments that we can return to ask not only where resistance lies, "[i]n what language will it be uttered?" (Ranciere, 1992, p. 58), and whether it will be an *"in-between* dialect" (Ibid., p. 58), but also what the relationship of such resistance is to desire and how we might attempt to think of the political field – here, a topology of queer politics – through moments of untranslatability, incommensurability, and different, often tendentious and contending logics? Would such a politics open itself up to different kinds of subjects, those included, those at the borders or margins, and those who are excluded, or outsided?

III. Interlude

Are Swapna and Sucheta queer political subjects like the ones I have tried to explore above? Where would their position be, as subjects who are incorporated into queer narratives, and as subjects who can *queer* the queer narrative hitherto presented? Are they subjects who author queer politics? Or are they queer subjects who are spoken for, represented, appropriated, and incorporated by the desire of queer politics? As we locate the centrality of identity and experience for the queer political subject, where do we find the subject of queer politics? And as we decentre the queer political subject, where do we find Swapna and Sucheta's place? Where would they fit within the discourse of human rights – as Third World victims, as tragic deaths, as lesbians first and humans second? What kind of work is needed to discover their desires, queer or otherwise, and where and how can we find their view of the world? Would that fit into the trajectory the queer political subject has charted for itself, the field of queer politics that it has built?

Perhaps we must first contend with their representations in order to attempt an answer . . . begin by mapping their story as it has been presented to us. Perhaps it will help us if we journey through their life in the narrative we already have of them, their tale told by others who have stood by them in their death. Perhaps, that story will also tell us something of truth, reveal something of desire, leave us with a remainder, a reminder . . . And as the story may shift in its re-telling, the truth might shift also, contingently . . .

Note

1 Since it remains true that feminism and queer activism have numerous strands to their politics, the question that emerges is about *which* strands of queer activism have incorporated *which* strands of feminism. In this work, I have engaged primarily with LBT collectives and tried to generate a narrative of queer politics in India from their perspective. That is, then, a strand of queer activism we can localize. As for feminism, and which feminism, there are liberal feminist, Marxist feminist, sometimes Dalit feminist perspectives that are seen as allies, albeit in-difference. So, perhaps these are the *feminisms* we must localize. And yet, *can* we localize (a methodological), or *should* we localize (an ethical question)? It seems that the implications of speaking from such situatedness are that LBT narratives can only represent LBT perspectives, and cannot offer to speak of other strands of queer organizing, and then, that LBT narratives from three cities can only speak of LBT organizing in those three cities, and then, that those narratives can only represent those who have spoken, and no one else in those cities. It is the essentialism of experience, only in a different manifestation. And yet, in queer politics, as in the women's movement, people are *spoken for* as well. A long engagement with either space will demonstrate how what seemed to be the mainstream voice of each space comes to be unravelled and becomes disaggregated. But, *it seems to be mainstream nonetheless*. And so, perhaps this is a question of our relation to knowledge production – can what is produced transcend its boundaries? – and as such, it is also a question of method.

... *She never used to hide anything from me. I also never hid anything from her. If I didn't see her for even a day, I used to feel like I have lost my entire world. When she and I would not meet some day, she would give me a letter. I would also give her a letter. Her satisfactions and problems, I used to care for. My satisfactions and problems, she used to care for. She was not really excited about studying. I would tell her to study all the time and convince her. After that, she was very involved in studying. Whatever she needed to study, she used to take from me. I also used to give her, I never used to say no. Her family members misunderstood this involvement of ours. Everyone said bad things and made up stories about me and Such, things that are beyond the acceptance of people. This is why all the marriage proposals I have received have been broken off. To this day, they are saying bad things about me and to me. I do not know where this ends. When they used to torture me and say bad things about me, and Such used to protest, they would scold her a lot. They did not accept that we liked-loved each other. They have always seen me in a bad way, been suspicious of me. That is why I have decided to leave this world and go.*

Swapna's letter, page 3.
Translation mine

4
INSIDE THE FOLD OF RE-PRESENTATIONS

The previous chapters, by presenting one narrative of queer politics in India and implicitly relating it to queer politics in other parts of the world, and then interrupting that already fragmented narrative by asking if such politics could be understood more robustly if we had a more comprehensive understanding of the political subject vis-à-vis psychoanalysis, perhaps manage to demonstrate how the topological field of queer politics is uneven in its solidarities, in who emerges as stakeholders and vanguards of power, and how they are able to do so. In this chapter, I hope to localize the focus on Swapna and Sucheta's suicide, the representation of that suicide, and what lies in the gap between those two truths. If Swapna and Sucheta are not like the subjects who author queer politics, but become subjects who are subjected to queer politics as their stories come to be represented and circulated in particular ways, then it becomes imperative to ask what happens as this process of representation unfolds.

What is known about Swapna, Sucheta, and their lives can be found in a letter Swapna left for her parents on the eve of their suicide; it can be heard in the narrative presented to us by *Sappho for Equality*, through their two fact-finding investigations into Swapna and Sucheta's village – Sonachura – in Nandigram, West Bengal; and, it can be seen in the documentary titled *Ebong Bewarish* (. . . *And the Unclaimed*), produced by *Sappho for Equality* in 2013. The incident, as the story goes, is clearly one about a lesbian couple committing suicide in the face of physical and psychological violence committed upon them and their bodies by their immediate community because of their desire to be with each other. And so, Swapna's and Sucheta's deaths fits into a larger trope of lesbian suicides in India, and comes to represent uncountable instances of lesbian suicides that remain undocumented and without proof. Swapna and Sucheta's suicide can also be seen as exceptional, in that their bodies were left unclaimed by their families, finally being burned by the local police after a week of their death, in a morgue along with other unidentified and unclaimed bodies. This act of unclaiming, perhaps an indicator that violence does not end with death and the body remains marked nonetheless, became an important motivation for *Sappho for Equality* to produce a documentary that told their story, interspersed by other narratives of violence on queer persons. In this reading, *Sappho for Equality* comes to *represent* Swapna and Sucheta's suicide, but also their reconstructed lives (after the event of their death). Therefore, what we know about Swapna and Sucheta until now is limited to a single story, a narrative that is represented as the violence of heteronormative sexuality.

According to Chow (2001), representation has traditionally been seen as divided between "absence and presence, primariness and secondariness, originality and derivation, authenticity and fakeness" (p. 39), which are moral oppositions, and as a result, value laden ones. This implicit morality inherent in the process of representation contributes to the problem of the a priori legitimacy of representing one's own experience, which Chow explains was seen as a counter to the difficulty of objective and accurate representation – a predicament that emerged due to these value laden binaries within which representation was being understood. She discusses how self-representation as ipso facto authentic and legitimate is problematic because historically, the "notion that a return to the self is 'emancipatory' is a myth that is as old as Enlightenment" (Ibid., p. 44). Following Foucault (1978), Chow explains how this myth produces the subject of confession, as opposed to a subject of truth – a subject who provides their experience as evidence. This, in turn, is tied to the illusion of a subject of absolute agency and freedom under Modernity, which disguises the effect of power on the subject and eludes the question of governmentality and subjectivation (and subjectivization). As I attempted to demonstrate in Chapter 3, to provide experience as evidence that presents itself as unmediated and opaque is directly linked to a sexual politics that sees queerness primarily as identity, and conceptualizes its demands for inclusion and human rights on the basis of envisioning that identity as personal choice and agency. Not only is such politics problematic, it also fails to have an accurate understanding of the subject, because "the self does not necessarily 'know' itself and cannot be reduced to the realm of rational cognition" (Chow, 2001, p. 46).

Another line of thought that highlights the dilemma of representation comes to us through subjects who cannot represent themselves. Spivak (1988) reveals them to be subaltern subjects, who – she states – cannot speak. According to Chow (2001), "if 'the subaltern cannot speak,' it is not only because representation involves institutional power but also because that power cannot be successfully resisted by turning representation toward *the self*" (p. 49). However, if self-representation and representation of others are both fraught with the difficulty of authenticity and legitimacy, then what is the way in which representation can take place by circumventing these problems? Further, who can represent – or stand in for – whom? For, in this case, the issue at stake is political representation (or, as Spivak puts it, representation by proxy), where the subject who represents stands in for the subject who is represented in a political and legal sense. The subject who represents (speaks for the represented subject) can do so through a transfer of power between subjects, and insofar as the subject who represents comes to acquire this power, it makes this process of representation (by proxy) deeply political.

I. Between subject and metonym

If we acknowledge that there is a politics of representation at play when the story of Swapna's and Sucheta's lives is told by *Sappho for Equality*, a group that finds itself in a position of power compared to Swapna and Sucheta in a segregated field of queer politics, perhaps there is another way to read Swapna's letter – not for its content, but for its form – in order to understand the place of the letter with respect to the suicide and its immediate surroundings. It is to shift the focus away from the words in the letter, and highlight the letter itself (that there was a letter, that it was not disappeared, that it said some things and hid others, that it said some things in a particular way) as saying something about the conditions of their suicide. It is to attempt to mark desire through the grammar of the letter, and try to reveal the structures of power that operate in the meaning making process of representation that has hitherto characterized their death.

It seems that to attend to the form of the letter is to place it in reference to a symbolic structure. For Lacan (1966/2006), to tend to the form of the letter – or the literality of the letter – was to place it within the structure of a language, such that the letter, symbolic as it was of the position of the subject caught in language, constituted the subject, rather than being constituted by it. Here, "language [*langue*] exists – to use it to signify *something altogether different* from what it says" (p. 421). As elaborated in Chapter 3, language represents the form of the letter, the logic of its grammar, and the way in which the subject is caught in language's structure. Further, within the Lacanian schema, the unconscious is structured like a language, and so its effects are felt in the constitution of the Lacanian subject. Since language – being in the realm of the symbolic and structuring the unconscious – has a function of always being Other than what it represents in speech, or in this case, writing, writing comes to encompass not only that which is written, but also that which is hinted at in the interstices between words. One way to engage with the form of the letter is to employ the use of the metonym (the part standing in for the whole), which Lacan (1957/2006) claimed was similar to Freud's concept of 'displacement'. This was because in both, metonym and displacement, there was a "transfer of signification . . . the unconscious' best means by which to foil censorship" (p. 425).

If this framework were to apply with respect to Swapna and Sucheta's suicide, it may be important to see the implications of the letter as a metonym standing in for their dead bodies. The letter would then no longer say what the words in the letter signify (to read the letter for its content is not enough); it uses language to say something *else*. This 'something else' is what circulates, without censorship, in a structure of violence (based on the censor) that does not claim their bodies after death. But then, *what* is being censored? What does it mean for the bodies to remain unclaimed? What is it that transfers from the bodies to the letter, and what remains behind – is un-transferable, unspeakable, un-writable? In the Lacanian frame, the answers to these questions seem to lie in desire, which in turn opens up the question of the Other, insofar as desire is oriented towards the Other, both emerging at the same moment in the subject.

For Lacan, the entry of desire is through a reading of the letter as a function of desire. The letter signals to desire, even emerges as a function of desire, but follows a trajectory that distracts from desire. It seems that this relation between desire and the letter is contradictory in this manner because the letter emerges in the symbolic register, which is not entirely congruous with speech or writing that manifests through the imaginary register, and in this passing of the signifier (or signifiers) from the symbolic to the imaginary, the letter distracts from desire, but in that distraction also provides a clue to where desire lies (not unlike the psychoanalytic symptom). This simultaneous hiding and revealing is the metonymic function of the letter; it reveals desire in a resignification that also serves as censor, thereby distracting from the trajectory and object of desire. Similarly, the letter, insofar as it symbolizes desire, hides and reveals desire. Further, desire is characteristically metonymic. It stands in for the unconstituted whole Other for the subject, towards which desire is directed, and as it returns, it becomes a metonym of the lack that is the only response of the Other to the subject (because the Other itself seems to be in a position of not being able to fulfill the subject's desire). Here, the desire that "presents itself as independent of the Law's mediation, because Law originates in desire" (Lacan, 1960/2006, p. 689), and the metonym, "which gives oppressed truth its field, [and] manifest[s] a certain servitude that is inherent in its presentation" (Lacan, 1957/2006, p. 423) come together to reveal that which is desired, to those who have the tools to see it.

At least three things are being said here with respect to the relation of the metonym to desire. First, the metonym is a message by the Other that passes through Law and undergoes resignification in order to expose itself in the imaginary, via a process of censorship and repression. Second, in the Lacanian frame, desire itself is metonymic in that it stands in for a whole – the Other – that is not fully amenable to being circumscribed in language. This implies that there is a fundamental irreducibility of desire to language; something is always amiss, not quite there, some*place* else. It also demonstrates how the metonymic function is one of combination, where it comes to represent the whole in part by combining the signifiers of the whole. Here, the metonym both presents and absents (Chiesa, 2007); it *represents* the Other, or perhaps the desire directed towards the Other, emerging because of the Other, and in this (re)presentation, it also absents the full force of desire. Third, the metonymic function of language allows desire to surpass censor and manifest itself *in a warped manner* in language. Since desire precedes the Law, and becomes the cause of the Law to institute itself on the subject, it is not fully amenable to language (the field in which Law upholds itself) in its pure form. The metonym, uniquely positioned to foil the censor by being subservient to it, therefore reveals some*thing* of desire.

With respect to the relation between desire, the unconscious, the signifier, repression (here, censor), and the metonymic function, Chiesa (2007) writes:

> Primal repression mythically occurs as soon as desire . . . is alienated in language, as soon as the individual subject uses language . . . which, in turn, marks the birth of the unconscious. Therefore, the fact that every signifier is doubly inscribed means simply that once one signifier has been repressed in the unconscious, all successive signifiers will be linked to the repressed signifier, the nucleus of repression, and will form chains *even though they are not themselves directly repressed*. The simple inscription of a signifier in the unconscious corresponds to a metonymic combination in the unconscious.
>
> (p. 55)

The metonym is therefore a function of displacement and combination that emerges in the interaction of two oscillations of the Lacanian subject: first, the tendentious see-saw (or Freudian *fort-da*) between desire and the Law that attempts to censor it; and, second, between the signifierization (the process of making a signifier) in the symbolic and the signification (the process of making meaning of the signifier) in the imaginary (Chiesa, 2007). If the metonym is indeed caught within these processes that structure the subject, and if we accept that Swapna's suicide letter can be seen as a metonym for the event of their death, where can we locate desire with respect to Swapna's letter? What is the place of desire in the event of the suicide, and that which precedes and follows it? Further, what of desire remains inarticulate, repressed? What does desire reveal in the surpassing of censorship? What is the place of the metonymic function in Swapna's letter, and what does its placement reveal about Swapna's and Sucheta's deaths?

To attempt to answer these questions might mean seeing Swapna's letter as the ground on which desire articulates itself in two places that thereafter lie *apposite* to each other. One is to see Swapna and Sucheta's desire, somewhat clearly demarcated, with respect to their relation and wanting to be together. This can be gauged from Swapna's letter, which articulates not only her desire for Sucheta, as well as Sucheta's desire for her, but perhaps more importantly, it communicates Swapna and Sucheta's desire to be with each other. The other is the desire of their immediate surroundings and community, which is invested in their separation while they are alive, and in their unclaiming when they are dead, something that is evidenced in Swapna's letter, as well as the documentary by *Sappho for Equality*. Perhaps this is the desire that operates in upholding the Law, because the Law is deeply invested in maintaining the reproductive heteronorm, a process that rests on placing outside its structure any other forms of desire (Butler, 1990).

If so, Swapna's suicide letter can be seen as a metonym in the face of this desire to uphold the Law; insofar as Swapna and Sucheta are made Other by the Law, it is the message of the Other that passes through Law via transmutation – it reveals the function of the Law. The function of the censor is perhaps where the letter, while clearly outlining Swapna and Sucheta's affection towards each other, remains ambiguous regarding any manifestation of sexual desire. As a member of *Sappho for Equality* says, "Swapna also was rather diplomatic in the letter. There is no mention of a physical relationship between them . . . perhaps we are assuming there was a physical relation, perhaps there was only desire . . ." (Personal correspondence, November, 2015). The content of the letter absents the bodies of Swapna and Sucheta. It may be that this absence is the subservience of the letter to the Law, which allows it to remain (instead of being burned, buried, or hidden by their families and immediate community) while their bodies go unclaimed. The presence of the letter, in turn, foils the Law by demonstrating what goes against it, and in that moment, surpasses it. If the letter is indeed a metonym, two questions remain unanswered. First, what is the structure within which the letter circulates and operates? Second, what is it that the letter tells us in the perspectival shift from its content to its form?

Letter, interstice, positions

In the Lacanian schema, the subject that holds an ambivalent duality in relation to Law and desire is caught, possibly, in a violent dialectic that seems inescapable. For Lacan, the entry of the subject into (the structure of) language – the very fact that perhaps distinguishes the animal from the human for Lacan, for language is what brings the subject into culture – is a violent process. From the moment of entry into language, the Lacanian subject remains trapped in many contradictory positions – between desire and the Law; between un-verbal (or pre-verbal) need and demand; between self and Other. These contradictions emerge from and perhaps also in (the unconscious, which is structured like a) language; consequently, the subject is never where it claims to be. It is *elsewhere*.

That which is always elsewhere, and the 'someplace else' nature of desire, perhaps come together to complicate the narrative of structural violence in Swapna and Sucheta's suicide. This structure simultaneously violates and creates the subject, and as such, it is a violent becoming, with its own effects. Swapna and Sucheta, insofar as their narrative of lesbian death in the face of the reproductive heteronorm stands true, were subject to the violence of its structure. That much, perhaps, is certain. However, to engage with this narrative of their death can open up questions such as: what are the effects of this narrative on Swapna and Sucheta's lives (which are reconstructed from the event of their death to begin with)? How does the trope of heterosexual violence on lesbian lives interact with other structural positions occupied by Swapna and Sucheta, such as their class and caste? In other words, what does the act of representing Swapna and Sucheta as lesbian lovers who commit suicide do to them, their materiality, and their other realities?

If we were to return to that which is contradictory in the field of Swapna's letter, which I have tried to establish as the tension between Law and desire on the symbolic register and in the realm of the unconscious, it might be possible to think that the violence is generated somewhere in between the two. Between the claim of the Law (a claim that institutes legitimacy perhaps) and the unclaimed elsewhere of desire, there is an inherent and structural violence. As such, it might be possible to think of the very *metonymization* of Swapna's letter as a result of violence. In this particular instance, then, what is the articulation of the Law, its claim, and its demand? The most obvious answer would be that the Law asserts itself through the demands of patriarchy and heterosexuality, that it insists on maintaining the reproductive heteronorm. This is the place where society and culture regulate desire (for here, desire does not necessarily subscribe to the norm, it is not straight, but follows a curved path, revolves around the *objet a*, never reaches a destination, is always already *queer*), and in that attempt at regulation, it seems, creates Swapna and Sucheta as Other via a process of exclusion. Structurally, Swapna and Sucheta are placed outside the field of what is legitimate, and the Law now acts on their desire in its illegitimacy. Swapna and Sucheta's immediate family and community demand that they follow the conventional path of lawful reproductive sexuality that assumes their gendered role as women. Sucheta is physically beaten and married to a man and Swapna is forbidden from seeing Sucheta in the hope of turning them away from their 'unnatural' desires. It seems entirely possible here to think of heterosexuality and patriarchy as symbolic structures that produce legitimate and illegitimate subjects by virtue of the subject's place in these structures. Even though there was no legal action taken against them in the chain of events that transpired, perhaps it is the symbolic, social power of authority and Law that lurks in the shadows of the community's unclaiming of their bodies; it features as an unspoken warning for those who are alive to not tread on those paths.

However, the way in which this structure is conceived, and the way in which Swapna and Sucheta are placed in it, constructs a narrative of their death as another lesbian suicide in India, and as such, seems to follow the logic of a universal narrative at the cost of obfuscating the particularities of Swapna's and Sucheta's lives. On one level, it seems possible to state that it is the very logic of heterosexuality and patriarchy that excludes Swapna and Sucheta from its structure, but at the same time, perhaps this claim erases the specificity of Swapna and Sucheta's suicide; it makes their suicide similar to all other lesbian suicides. As someone from *Sappho for Equality* says,

> something has to be there that enables me to end my life . . . we have years of conditioning on how to survive . . . to not survive by choice is not so easy . . . it is a way to make yourself heard, especially when you are leaving a suicide note . . . it was not about "I loved a girl and they didn't let me live with the girl so I committed suicide". It was a story, a journey . . .
> *(Personal correspondence, November, 2015)*

There is context, at least in the form of geography, economy, caste, and history, in relation to which Swapna's and Sucheta's deaths can be placed that cannot, it seems, be entirely accounted for by the story of Swapna and Sucheta as narrated by *Sappho for Equality*. This is not to deny the violence of reproductive heterosexuality on Swapna and Sucheta, nor is it to negate the terror that colours queer lives and their many realities. At the same time, perhaps to document Swapna and Sucheta's multiple lived realities within unfulfilled lesbian desire is to leave something incomplete. The assumption here – the solid field within which *Sappho for Equality* place their intervention – is that it was the primacy of heterosexuality that produced the violence.

And yet, it is not only heterosexuality and its censor that is at work here; to see their death as such is to continue to interpret their suicide (and in retrospect, their lives) for its content, and not for its form. There are numerous positions Swapna and Sucheta occupied – gender, caste, economy, and geography being only a few of them. To read their death as a lesbian suicide, while entirely true, also produces its own effects that erase, or at least subsume, these other parts of their selves and represent them as lesbian women, and lesbian women only. In the Lacanian schema, it seems that the metonymic function of the letter also ensures that what is metonymized will consequently become linked to chains of signifiers, even if that signifying chain was not subject to repression (Chiesa, 2007). Perhaps what this implies is that, in the process of metonymization, the function of the secret now becomes associated with other chains of signifiers, all of which attempt to distract from desire, but are also, consequently, symptoms of that desire. That which is hidden, and in this case, relegated to an aporetic place (by virtue of death) can then possibly be reached by tracing multiple signifying chains to the point where they intersect; within multiple meanings that are generated in this process, something that was hidden might reveal itself.

With respect to Swapna's and Sucheta's deaths, another line of signification and meaning making could perhaps be through the lens of gender. In the narrative that comes to us through *Sappho for Equality* it has been acknowledged that Swapna and Sucheta were in a position of double effacement because of them being gendered women and oriented sexually as lesbians. However, it is possible that the role of gender in their lives goes beyond the inequality that one faces by virtue of being a woman. For example, as someone from *Sappho for Equality* says,

> when their bodies were found, one of them was wearing a trouser . . . but the photographs in the newspapers showed them wearing a *salwar* . . . you couldn't claim them, you couldn't burn their bodies, but you could change their trouser into *salwar* . . .
> *(Personal correspondence, November, 2015)*

It seems that Sucheta was wearing trousers typically worn by men when she and Swapna committed suicide. What remains unclear is how and at what point in the course of events someone changed those trousers into a *salwar*, a garment typically worn by women. Yet, there is no mention of this cross-dressing in the documentary *Ebong Bewarish*. Someone involved in both fact-finding investigations says, "the men in the village kept saying the girls in the village don't have short hair, they wear *sarees* . . . I think they were very ashamed of what happened" (Personal correspondence, November, 2015). Is it possible that the silence on the part of Sucheta's family, which numerous members of *Sappho for Equality* attributed to pressure exerted upon them by their immediate community, was not about lesbian desire alone, but also about a biological woman's desire to cross-dress at the very least, or about her wish to see herself as a man at the most extreme?

When Spivak (1988) describes Bhuvaneshwari Bhaduri's death, she emphasizes that the subaltern woman is in a position of such untranslatability and mis-representation that the only way in which she can articulate herself is through death, her body becoming the text she leaves behind. In this instance, even the bodily text Sucheta desired to leave behind seems to have been effaced. Not only were Swapna and Sucheta not claimed by their families and community in their death, their bodies were further resignified after their suicide. The desire of the community not to come face to face with the desire of its Other was persistent; death was not the moment in which the game of representation and resignification came to an end. There was it seems, at best, a metonymic cut.

Further, in the first fact-finding investigation conducted by *Sappho for Equality* (available in their archives in Kolkata), there is what seems to be an insignificant discovery – Sucheta's husband, whom she was forcibly married to, had attempted to commit suicide, unsuccessfully, after getting married. This was never again discussed in the subsequent investigation, nor was it an important feature of the resulting documentary. There was only one mention of Sucheta's husband in the interviews I conducted, when someone from *Sappho for Equality* said, "it was very difficult to see Sucheta's husband. Nothing was his fault, and because he was forced to marry her, his life was also destroyed . . ." (Personal correspondence, November, 2015). We do not know why he attempted to commit suicide, what his motivations were, whether it was because he could no longer ignore the relationship between Swapna and Sucheta, whether it was that he had been forced into the marriage himself, whether it was that he began to suspect Sucheta was not someone to fit the stereotypical feminine role, or if it was something else entirely. There is no certitude to be found in anticipating how Sucheta's husband might have come to face Sucheta as his Other, and what manifestation it might have taken, what event it may have led to. The only thing that it perhaps tells us is that the place of violence is somewhat displaced from what we understood earlier in the event of Swapna's and Sucheta's deaths.

While one kind of meaning making can take place by following the play of gender and its place in Swapna and Sucheta's suicide, another kind of meaning might be made by entering through the question of class, where it may be helpful to see how Swapna's and Sucheta's economic conditions impacted their lives and deaths. Swapna's letter talks at length about the struggle for education in a household with meagre resources. Perhaps an interesting intersection between Swapna and Sucheta's economic condition and their suicide can be found here, where someone involved in the fact-finding investigation from *Sappho for Equality* says, "the bodies were still lying in the morgue, even though the police had offered them [their families] assistance and money to burn their bodies . . ." (Personal correspondence, November, 2015). What is the relation of Swapna's and Sucheta's families and community with money, and how are they placed within the economic field? Are they themselves subaltern figures, insofar as they are acted upon by the market, but cannot act upon the market themselves? And how, if at all, is this related to Swapna and Sucheta, their embodiment and articulation of sexuality? It seems that even within what can possibly be a subaltern group or community, there is scope for further subalternization, as if so, *what* of (queer) sexuality is that which is always effaced, always put outside, always the Other?

Yet another point of reference to enter into Swapna and Sucheta's suicide could be to raise the question of caste; Swapna and Sucheta were both lower caste women, presumably living in an entirely lower caste community. What role did their caste have to play in their deaths, if it had any role to play at all? Each community has its own relation to bodies and its own rituals and collective beliefs about death, which are in turn mediated by their geographical location and occupation. As such, what can we find by exploring Swapna and Sucheta's suicide in relation to their caste? Is there something specific about their geographical location that can also help make meaning of their place as non-normative women and reconstruct something of their lives? Someone from *Sappho for Equality* said,

> this is the same Nandigram where we have dug up graves and CPI(M) and Trinamool [two competing left-leaning political parties who have a stronghold in West Bengal] have fought over who would claim those bones . . . and in the same Nandigram, this issue could be suppressed . . . it is the same Medinipur [another district close to Nandigram] that was at the forefront of the freedom struggle, where women's activism was prominent . . .
>
> *(Personal correspondence, November, 2015)*

Perhaps it is the nature of Swapna and Sucheta's unclaiming in the history and geography of contested claims that may reveal something to us about the constitution of (queer) sexuality in the community, and its importance in relation to other political movements. What does the shame and silence around sexuality tell us in a place where there have been almost too many words on labour, on politics, perhaps even on the emancipation of women?

Finally, but perhaps not exhaustively, to focus on the two-ness of the suicide might also tell us something about the nature of Swapna and Sucheta's suicide as a *lesbian* suicide. When six women tried to commit suicide together in Jamboni, West Midnapur, West Bengal in February, 2015, this incident was not seen as an obvious case of lesbian suicide. As someone from *Sappho for Equality* said,

> We do not actually know if there is any sexual desire at work in this group suicide at Jamboni . . . They talk about the unnatural bonding or friendship between these girls . . . there is primary data we have, that this a very core bonding they had, it was unnatural friendship, an intense friendship . . .
> *(Personal correspondence, November, 2015)*

Even though the terms used to describe the relationship between Swapna and Sucheta and these girls remained the same – 'unhealthy bonding' and 'abnormal togetherness' (as found in newspaper articles reviewing both incidents) – something about the nature of this suicide did not signify it as a lesbian suicide, as Swapna and Sucheta's suicide did. Is this an indicator, then, of how two women committing suicide together is seen as necessarily *homosexual*? Without erasing desire between Swapna and Sucheta, can we ask whether the nature of that desire was homosexual, and homosexual in the way we have come to understand it today, under the aegis of Modernity, as localized, interiorized, and something entirely distinct from friendship, as separate even from eroticism (a word of the past)? When we claim that Swapna and Sucheta's suicide was a *lesbian* suicide, what is the signification of the term 'lesbian', and how are we certain that they were 'lesbians' in the way we are signifying them as such? As someone from *Sappho for Equality* said, "what does it mean to say 'lesbian couple suicide'? And was it only 'lesbian couple suicide?' . . . So was it only a question of sexuality? Or was it a much larger question . . ." (Personal correspondence, November, 2015).

Can Swapna and Sucheta speak?

The task here is not so much to answer the riddle of Swapna and Sucheta's suicide. It is, instead, to explore what lies in the folds of what is represented. In doing so, the attempt is that of decentring the assumptions of the narrative without reducing its importance. It remains vital to highlight a lesbian suicide that remained unclaimed in Nandigram, and the effects it produced, the suffering it caused, and the pain and anger it generated in those who first discovered it, and later, in those who learned of it. However, to unravel the assumptions behind representation is to call into question the modes of power that might operate in the process of representation itself. It is to return to the question of whether Swapna and Sucheta could speak, even in their death. It is to ask whether portraying Swapna and Sucheta as a lesbian couple that committed suicide is itself a process that effaces parts of their lives, and as such, is a process where power is still not on their side. It is to raise the question of representation, and ask whether the way in which *Sappho for Equality* stands in for Swapna and Sucheta, as well as the violence they were subjected to, is a process of proxy where *Sappho for Equality* also claims their voice in a process that displaces them in some way.

Is it possible that in this instance, even in the best intentions, *Sappho for Equality*'s assumption – that this was a lesbian suicide – closes off certain aspects of Swapna's and Sucheta's lives, bars certain narratives from emerging? Does the burden of lesbianism now weigh heavily enough on Swapna and Sucheta to metonymize them further, even in the most well-meaning narrative, enough to make them the objects of a politics that was far away from them when they were alive? Does an a priori knowledge get constructed, to obstruct other orientations of their lives, other directions that were not *sexual*, but might still reveal something of *sexuality*? Is it that in the aftermath of Swapna's and Sucheta's deaths, they are made into particular subjects, lesbian women silenced forever, but who must now be spoken for, and through that proxy, be subjected to a certain kind of politics, even if they may not necessarily have had any voice in that politics had they been alive? As someone from *Sappho for Equality* says, "What cost will Swapna and Sucheta have to pay to belong to our movement? And on the other hand, what cost will we have to pay to open ourselves up to them? Are we ready to share?" (Personal correspondence, November, 2015).

To ask these questions is not to undermine the necessity of *Sappho for Equality's* intervention, but to attempt to explore the constructions and omissions of the process through which *Sappho for Equality* came to stand in for Swapna and Sucheta. And yet, along with these questions, perhaps we need to ask another one: would it be possible to imagine another mode of representation in a queer politics that is driven towards inclusion through the legal discourse of human rights, and as such, hinges on representation? In a politics that does not necessarily change the structure of oppression, would there be a way in which Swapna and Sucheta could be seen as subjects who authored their own politics, rather than becoming subjects who were subjected to queer politics? Was there another path available to *Sappho for Equality* that would bring Swapna and Sucheta's suicide to light without co-opting their narrative and re-presenting it as a lesbian suicide alone? Given the political framework within which *Sappho for Equality* finds itself, one can argue that to represent Swapna and Sucheta's suicide like they did was a necessary straightening of forever Borromean subjectivities – one that was required to further the agendas of queer politics, but also one that creates a false equivalence between *Sappho for Equality* and Swapna and Sucheta.

As elaborated in Chapter 3, if the structuring principle remains untouched, margins simply reconfigure to include those at its border-zones, while creating newer borders, at its own costs. Further, if power is generative and repressive at multiple sites for the same subject, then it might mean that the same subject who is oppressed can be oppressive in turn. This is akin to the framework that segregates power as margins of margins, and if this logic of power holds, then perhaps it is possible to think of Swapna and Sucheta as either farther away from the margins than those who represent them, or as entirely outside the structure within which those who represent them exist (albeit at the margins themselves). In addition, it seems that this understanding of power as it creates margins of margins remains antithetical to an understanding of politics that is based on marginalization, and the drive to escape that marginalization in a move towards equality through legal human rights discourse, primarily because that discourse equalizes all marginalities at best, and quantifies them as more marginal or less marginal at worst. Further, within the collectivization that takes place because of marginalization – within a marginalized group – differences are erased as a representational identity marker becomes significant to collectivization. To think of margins of margins is, possibly, to move away from such frameworks of centrality and marginalization, dominance and subordination, in favour of over-determined interstices and subject formations that come together to produce the margins of margins.

If we accept that Swapna and Sucheta might occupy this place of the margins of margins, then they can be seen as positioned as the "symptoms of discourse" (Chaudhury, Das, & Chakrabarty, 2000), such that there is a particular relationship with discursive productions – one determined by the dialectic of the surface and the secret. Here, an erasure of difference that hides Swapna and Sucheta's position (in order to claim them within discourse, even if at its margins) can perhaps be linked to the assumption that comes from the "myth of knowingness" (Lear, 1998) that is reproduced by the naturalization of experience as the basis of representative politics within a field of marginalizations. It is as if the voice of a kind of queer politics *knows* Swapna and Sucheta's story. This, in turn, produces a priori knowledges that do not cognize "that the process of construction and functioning of this knowledge requires itself to be outside discourse, as it were, that presumes an a-priori truth that it merely, and it alone, can represent" (Achuthan, 2001, p. 65). Queer politics becomes, then, Swapna and Sucheta's experiential ally in a way that creates a closure where the experience (of lesbian life and death) *lies*.

This process in which a priori knowledge reigns as untainted truth creates an object out of the subject it is directed towards. This objectification is what contributes to the process of making the Other (speak through) a metonym – the function of the metonym is to make a part (object) stand in for the whole (subject). The knowledge process is what creates the conditions in which the subject can only respond as object. It is here that Swapna and Sucheta find themselves caught in another metonymization – a making Other not only by their community, but also by those who seek to re-present them in their deaths, albeit through different processes, in separate modes, with distinct intentions. If we find Swapna and Sucheta metonymized not only through their unclaiming and disavowal by their community, but also in a narrative constructed by queer politics that seemed to claim and represent them, where is it that they will be able to represent themselves? When, under which conditions, given what kind of developments, can Swapna and Sucheta speak?

II. Hesitations

Perhaps to answer these questions is to return to the question of representation, a move that must now be informed by not only the political weight of representation for the subject of politics (or the subject who is subjected to politics), but also the psychoanalytic or psychic dimensions of the subject. I have already tried to highlight the problems of political representation, which remains caught between authenticity and inauthenticity, and reproduces the centred subject with illusions (or perhaps, delusions) of authority and agency. However, what happens to representation when the subject is psychoanalytically in question? In other words, what happens to self-representation in a Lacanian subject who is itself undone by language, ambivalently swaying between contentious poles, essentially decentred and contending with its own agency and the agency of the unconscious?

According to Cuellar (2010), it might be productive to think of representation in tandem with the three registers of the imaginary, symbolic, and real, the last of which possibly eludes representation. If it is possible that it is the realm of the symbolic in which signifierization happens and the imaginary is the field in which meaning is made, then it logically follows that symbolic representation contends with the unconscious subject, while imaginary representation deals with the subject as socio-cultural object. Here, symbolic representation deals with the subject of the unconscious, for whom knowledge is alienated insofar as it emerges in relation to the Other. As such, the representative of the subject might be its Other. The imaginary representation is akin to object (as opposed to subject) perhaps because it is here that the alienated subject manifests itself, and is therefore not the subject, but a part of the subject that is made meaning of – a meaning that is alienated from the subject of the unconscious. In other words, the subject of imaginary representation is represented (as object, or in part) by the symbolic representation of the subject. In Cuellar's (2010) terms the subject "*is represented by what [s]he represents*, but *[s]he is not what [s]he represents*" (p. 215). This is also because between the symbolic and imaginary representations of the subject, there is an absence of the real subject, or rather, the real of the subject.

In such a framework, insofar as 'queer' (or 'lesbian', 'gay', 'bisexual', 'trans' . . .) might be a symbolic signifier that orients a person's sexuality perhaps in ways that move beyond their object choice and sexual behaviour, the subject is represented by their queerness, while representing queerness themselves. However, the subject is not only queer, not queer only, not necessarily queer, not queer like another subject uttering and adopting 'queer', but somewhere else, something other than. The queer of the subject is still a symbolic mask of the queer subject, but all the while the subject eludes full representation. Something is elided here; we are always a little amiss when representing ourselves, representing others, and as such, something is always a little remiss in representation. As someone involved in the documentary *Ebong Bewarish* says,

> [Over time] I have kept feeling that I did not know Swapna and Sucheta . . . it is really important to know them, recognize them . . . I kept feeling that I was doing something wrong, making a mistake . . . I keep feeling that I cannot catch their narrative [in its entirety] . . . I cannot escape this, I keep feeling I am unable to represent them . . . I keep feeling this failure . . .
>
> *(Personal correspondence, November, 2015)*

Perhaps it is the trap of representation that is being alluded to here. Swapna and Sucheta, despite their lesbianism, despite queer activist discourse, despite the intentions of those involved in finding them, are still absent while having been presented, or re-presented. Amid this absent presence, inside the surface story and illusory truth of representation, what is it that remains amiss, and how is it that we might remain true to its absence? Is it possible to remain attuned to what lies inside the folds of representation, such that it can perhaps counter the effects of its truth, whose logic is kept outside what it reproduces?

For it is not that those who represented Swapna and Sucheta are without their own doubts, their own hesitations. According to someone who was involved in both fact-finding investigations in Swapna and Sucheta's village, their position of power as women of economic and social capital by virtue of them working in an NGO was apparent to the villagers, and also obvious to them. She says,

> Looking back, I think of the way in which the men made us leave . . . we were in power positions, and yet they had managed to make us leave, so what could they have done to Swapna and Sucheta and their families? It would have been impossible for the families to resist them . . . To have claimed the bodies would mean acceptance somewhere, and to not is to make a point, that if you do this, nobody will claim you . . .
>
> *(Personal correspondence, November, 2015)*

Because of their status as outsiders to the village community, the fact-finding team was reacted to in a hostile manner during their second visit, and their economic and social capital was not enough to protect them. As such, we can ask whether there is a relation between their acknowledgement of social and economic capital, which functions almost like an a priori assumption, and the other seemingly a priori assumption of knowing Swapna's and Sucheta's deaths as a lesbian suicide and believing that there was nothing new to learn there.

However, in light of this insight about the kind of pressures that must perhaps be at work within the community, some members of *Sappho for Equality* questioned the mode of their entry into the village, especially during the second fact-finding investigation, which took place 9 months after Swapna and Sucheta's death. According to one member,

> If today Swapna and Sucheta happened . . . we will think again twice or thrice . . . Now when I see myself, I think I have intruded . . . We had all the right reasons, we were all emotionally devastated . . . but now I'm questioning my right reasons, my reasoning . . . We still use that film [*Ebong Bewarish* . . .] . . . and people really connect to violence . . . but when you look at that from a distance, as a person . . . I really have difficulty . . . This is not just ethics . . . we did not have a base. We did not initiate a dialogue . . . We just came from a space and entered another space, not explaining ourselves . . . This is not the way it should be . . . What happened after we came back? We didn't do anything. We could have thought of other organizations working there . . . if we really wanted to work there, we could have created some familiarity . . . The going was inevitable, perhaps it was needed . . . and the connections we are now making through the film are very important . . . at the same time, this is a lesson for us to learn as well . . .
> *(Personal correspondence, November, 2015)*

What is being questioned here is the mode of operation, the way in which *Sappho for Equality* entered the village, which was for them an alien space, like they were alien to it. Perhaps just by virtue of their rural location, Swapna and Sucheta were not subjects about whom there was nothing new to learn. At least two things are important here. First, the emotional charge that *Sappho for Equality* and its members feel when faced with such a suicide – the loss, the hopelessness, the sorrow, the rage, and the unsurety. Second, their desire to prevent such fatalities in the face of something as drastic, incontrovertible, and aporetic as suicide. This helplessness informs the sentiment of almost all the members of *Sappho for Equality* with respect to Swapna and Sucheta; to have lost these lives, so close and yet so far from Kolkata's metropolis is not easy for those who came together to fight the isolation that was caused by their desire.

And yet, this helplessness, hesitations and doubts do not seem to make their way into the field of queer politics, nor into its discursive language, that *Sappho for Equality* contributes to. It is almost as if, as individuals imbricated in queer politics, there are certain affects and relations that are considered to exceed the boundaries of the field of queer politics, or are seen as other than what queer politics should be. It is perhaps that the individual who does politics and the field of politics are distinct, but interrelated. Here, the individual who is the subject and author of queer politics is caught between the dialectic of the imaginary and the symbolic registers, and it seems that it is the former that is the field of queer politics, and all affect, hesitation, and helplessness is relegated (or disavowed) to the realm of the psychoanalytic symbolic. A politics that is restricted to the imaginary register is perhaps a politics that has a linear account of time; the past is to be historicized, and in the future there lies the imagination of utopia. It is in this distance between the past and the present, and the present and the future, that political action seems to become imbricated in a pressure of certainty, of anticipating concrete, visible revolutions, and can then no longer allow for any moments of hesitation, uncertainty, and often, questioning; as a result, queer narratives are straightened, and such straightening is considered necessary.

And yet, so much of how any political movement begins is about the affect and desire that is involved in bringing people together, and through dialogue, debate, and dissent, reaching some semblance of collective action. Somewhere in the process of becoming a political collective, it seems, a political discourse emerges that necessitates the division between emotion and political action, between doubts and anxieties that are inherent to any political decision or action, and what is believed to be necessary for doing politics – a certain linearity, or, a linear certainty. Arendt (2005) argues that politics is precisely that which occurs between people, and so, it may be that it is these moments that are full of debate, hesitation, and doubt, that prove to be productive markers of how any political movement emerges, evolves, progresses, and dies. Perhaps it is these moments of emotion that have hitherto been seen as counterproductive to politics that demonstrate for us the limits, failures, and also strongholds of what we theorize as the political today. But then, what would such a rethinking of the limits of politics entail? Would it shift the impetus of politics from the certainty of utopias (for which the political subject often pays innumerable costs, and blindly so) to the uncertainty of temporality and subjectivity, through which more robust understandings of collectivity can emerge?

Derrida, in a documentary (Ziering and Kofman, 2002), distinguishes between a predictable future, here, the future that queer politics is engaged with, a future that revolves around anticipatable legal reforms, and an unpredictable future, which he calls *l'avenir*, a future that is yet to come. It is in this latter sense of time that the Other resides, whose arrival is always unexpected. And it is with an unexpected future that we might find a relation to the symbolic register. The register shifts as we move between the imaginary subject of queer politics and the symbolic subject of psychoanalysis, and in this move, there is a shift in the language of the political, the way in which resistance is articulated. This is a shift that requires the work of translation, a moment of slippage that perhaps maintains the division between the individual subject of politics who always seems to carry a certain excess, or irreducibility, and the larger political field. But it is also this same shift that might provide moments of resistance that cannot be colonized by power.

Given this division, and the inability of the dialectic to piece together the divide between the politics, psychoanalysis, and language, what are the ways in which the queer subject could imagine a politics of queerness that was amenable to hesitations, limits, helplessness, and affect? According to someone from *Sappho for Equality*,

> I think this is where we are losing out . . . we are unable to see . . . we are constantly making gender-sexuality an extremely closed space, where we are looking at gender as male/female/Trans, instead of a social organization or even a hierarchization of bodies and beings . . . we are making gender-sexuality extremely essentialized categories . . . We are unable to move out of such formulations in any way at all . . .
> *(Personal correspondence, November, 2015)*

If this is the trap of queer politics on the subject, what possible modes are available that provide an exit?

III. Interlude

As we move from the various imbrications of representation in Swapna and Sucheta's suicide and turn to its implications, Swapna and Sucheta remain missing. They disappear somewhere inside the folds of what represents them, and their disappearance reveals the contours of queer politics. Perhaps Swapna and Sucheta's disappearance is queer politics' symptom. Perhaps it reveals queer politics' desire as incongruent with Swapna's and Sucheta's subjectivities. Perhaps it hides Swapna and Sucheta for what they truly mean for queer activism. Is it possible to think of

Swapna and Sucheta outside the margins of queer politics, beyond its language, as figures that elude full representation? And if Swapna and Sucheta are only represented in queer politics in part, as metonymized objects, does it make them Other than queer activism, or queer politics' Other? And yet, these questions are all hinged on the nature of queer politics, the boundaries of its discourse ... Where are Swapna and Sucheta? Who are they as subjects, as subjects whose sexuality we have called into question? Does their sexuality allow us to bring it in relation with subalternity?

... *We both like-love each other so much, that even today we do not know if we will ever be able to forget. If I am alive, I will never be able to forget her. She will also not be able to forget me. The people of this world are never ready to accept the like-love that is between us. They tried very hard to create problems between us, but they did not succeed. They will never be able to succeed either. She didn't like this boy, but her Baba and Ma forcibly wanted to marry her off to him. That time, she and I were very close. Everyone used to think I have told her to not marry. But believe me, I swear to god that I have never said anything to her about that relationship. I only used to tell her to study, but everyone began to misunderstand me. That is why they all used to say horrible things about me. But Such never said anything about that. A few days later, when I would find out what they were saying and ask Such why she didn't tell me, she used to say, "What if you stop talking to me, stop meeting me? That is why I haven't told you". When they used to cross a line, then she would tell me. After a point of time, they tried to stop our relation. They used to say bad things about me and Such, things which are never even possible. I never had a bad relation with her. I like-love her a lot, and she also likes-loves me a lot. We will not manage to live without each other. That is why those who are responsible for our deaths, god will never forgive them.*

Swapna's letter, page 4.
Translation mine

5
TOWARDS SEXUAL SUBALTERN SUBJECTS

Until now, I have tried to establish that Swapna and Sucheta – as well as other subjects who occupy positions like theirs – can be spoken for by queer politics in India, can perhaps be addressed by feminism in indirect ways, but cannot represent themselves in the discourses that are weighted with power in queer politics in India.

Considering its many voices, subjectivities, and geographies, it is difficult to claim any kind of singularity to queer politics in India. This might be because there is no big Other of queer politics, which implies that queer politics does not address One Other, does not orient itself in one direction, giving queer politics a productive opening of radical difference within itself (Penney, 2014). This also moves away from assuming an always already present solidarity among the many authors and voices of queer politics. At the same time, there might be a "latent transferential fantasy" (Ibid. p. 68) on the part of queer politics to imagine an:

> idealized queer big Other, who would bestow legitimacy on the various non-heterosexual communities, [that] is increasingly the middle-class or upper-middle-class, elite educated, savvy consumer, [who is] almost always located in the global North, or else the 'securitized' enclaves of the megalopolises of what we used to call the third world.
>
> *(Ibid. p. 68)*

Such transference reveals the symptomatic nature of queer politics in India that is driven towards globalization, equality and human rights, and inclusion. What this transferential relation does to not only the big Other, but also the global North is that it effaces queer subjects (in the global North as well as the Third World) who are not middle- or upper-middle-class, who are not educated, or not in a position to be consumers. If this interpretation were to hold true, we could claim that the queer politics and activism that is stuck in such transference is a politics that can easily become blind to race, religion, caste, and political economy; this is politics that lends itself to violent constructions of nationhood and development (Gross, 2017; Upadhyay & Ravecca, 2017).

Swapna and Sucheta are most decidedly not such subjects. They do not have access to any kind of capital it seems – economic, social, or cultural; the power that decides authority in queer politics is not on their side. As such, it is their effacement that must be understood in order to move beyond an imaginary transferential queer politics and attempt to reach a politics that can generate a revolution in subjectivity, one that breaches the symbolic. This might mean not only generating newer forms of meaning making for the signifier 'queer', which are more attentive to Swapna, Sucheta, and other effaced subjects that are left out of queer politics' transference, but also entail finding newer languages with which to articulate desire, and as such, write newer histories that are methodologically oriented queer (Ahmed, 2006), voicing histories of contemporary moments haunted by queer spectres (Freccero, 2007). But first, it would perhaps mean answering the question of what kind of subjects Swapna and Sucheta might be and what would it mean to reclaim them. How would we orient histories queerly to discover Swapna and Sucheta, speaking to us through those histories? And so, I wonder if Swapna and Sucheta can be sexual subaltern subjects. But then, what would it mean to be a sexual subaltern subject? How would it differ from the subaltern subject as we have hitherto invoked it?

I. A brief tracing of the subaltern in Indian contexts

The subaltern figure as a theoretical and political intervention has a particular history in the Indian subcontinent, one that cannot be written without engaging with the work of the Subaltern Studies Collective (henceforth, SSC). It seems that the 'subaltern' emerged in the Indian subcontinent for the first time in the early 1980s, and could be seen as having been inaugurated within the field of history, particularly the history of India's colonization. The conceptual figure of the 'subaltern' was posited as absent from any form of colonial or nationalist history writing about the Indian nation. Both versions of history writing were categorized as 'elite', because they signified the history of "*dominant groups, foreign as well as indigenous*" (Guha, 1982, p. 8). Those who constituted the elite were not a homogenous category in terms of class or race, but were stratified and diverse based on regional socio-economic developments. The subaltern, then, came to be defined in difference from the elite, where "[t]he social groups and elements included in this category represent *the demographic difference between the total Indian population and those whom we have described as the 'elite'*" (Ibid., p. 8). For Prakash (1994), "[t]he term 'subaltern', drawn from Antonio Gramsci's writings, refers to subordination in terms of class, caste, gender, race, language, and culture and was used to signify the centrality of dominant/dominated relationships in history" (p. 1477). Due to the heterogeneity of both categories – the subaltern and the elite – some groups and classes who were subaltern in one instance, "could under certain circumstances act for the 'elite' ... *not in conformity to interests corresponding truly to their own social being*" (Guha, 1982, p. 8). It was, then, up to the subaltern historian to gauge when and where the subaltern was manifested in history.

The subaltern between absence and presence in history and politics

This task seemed to be a difficult one, since one fundamental characteristic of the subaltern was that he was absent from dominant modes of history.[1] For Guha (1982), this absence was caused by an orientation of historiography that had a "narrow and partial view of politics to which it is committed by virtue of its class outlook" (p. 3). In other words, the absence of the subaltern was due to a limited understanding of politics in the field of (colonial and nationalist) historiography that understood politics as a vertical process of mobilization and intervention. It was a bias in terms of class that blinded these historiographies to the presence of the subaltern, who formed an autonomous domain that existed "parallel to the domain of elite politics" (Ibid., p. 4). Since both versions of historiography dealing with the Indian nation were oriented towards, and based in, elite perspectives, the subaltern was absent from their view. Further, the autonomy of the subaltern, or its independence from the elite, was compounded by the fact that subaltern mobilization was a horizontal process that was seen as "relatively more violent ... [and] more spontaneous"

(Ibid., pp. 4–5) than elite politics. Subaltern politics was theorized as unified in its resistance to elite domination, and it did so with something akin to a *different language of resistance* that elite versions of historiography did not see. This was because both nationalist and colonialist historiography, for Guha (1989), put subaltern resistance "*firmly outside politics*" (p. 299). The subaltern had a logic of its own that was distinct from the logic of the elite, and as such, their history was different from elite history.

In this understanding of the subaltern, it seems that not only does the subaltern have claims to a history different from that of the elite, but its difference from the elite also emerges in its modes of resistance, which are absented from what elite history considered the field of politics, or the domain of politics. For Guha (1989), this was made possible through what he calls "two vanishing tricks" (p. 300); the first of these was to consider political resistance as a vertical process in which mobilization occurs through a top-down mode such that only vertical alliances are considered political, and horizontal alliances — here, alliances among the same group — are considered local, and therefore, at best seen as "pre-political" (Ibid., p. 301).

For Guha, this was the second way in which subaltern resistance was outsided from politics; by seeing their ideology and alliances based on caste, religion, regional language, etc., as cultural elements, and not political ones (Guha, 1989). In this way, subaltern solidarity and ideology were removed from what was understood as politics, such that they could only be read as 'acts of spontaneous insurgency'. Compounding this problem was that, while instances of spontaneous subaltern insurgency were numerous, the subaltern classes themselves were "still not sufficiently mature in the objective conditions of its social being and in its consciousness as a class-for-itself, nor was it firmly allied with the peasantry" (Guha, 1982, p. 6). This disaggregated form of insurgency — or, the multiple manifestations of horizontal alliance — allowed the subaltern to remain as if invisible and powerless in the elite history of the Indian nation under colonialism.

The absencing of the subaltern from history and its resistance from politics had consequences for the figure of the subaltern when he was (re)presented in historiography. The subaltern's presence in historiography was to "give the lie to the myth . . . of peasant insurrections being purely spontaneous and unpremeditated affairs" (Guha, 1983, p. 1). This led to historical writing that "has been content to deal with the peasant rebel merely as an empirical person or member of a class, but not as an entity whose will and reason constituted the praxis called rebellion" (Ibid.,

p. 2). In other words, both nationalist and colonial historiography created the figure of the subaltern as one devoid of Reason, such that "insurgency is regarded as *external* to the peasant's consciousness and Cause is made to stand in as a phantom surrogate of Reason, the logic of that consciousness" (Ibid., p. 3). The subaltern was constructed as a figure that was not a conscious political subject, but one who would spontaneously erupt into violent agitation as an immediate response towards economic or political deprivations – such moments were not seen as carefully planned resistance with intention or ideology behind them. Simply put, the subaltern was constructed as a figure that had no stakes in the politics of his times. For Guha (1983), this was a 'mythification' of the subaltern, in which the subaltern himself contributed, in all likelihood because to resist was to "destroy many of those familiar signs which he had learned to read and manipulate in order to extract a meaning out of the harsh world around him and live with it" (p. 1). In such a reading, the risk of resistance was very high for the subaltern, and in the face of this risk, insurgency could not have been merely spontaneous, rather, requiring premeditation and organization.

In dividing the subaltern from Reason, elite historiography constructed the subaltern as a figure without consciousness. Here, consciousness seems to be understood only through the elite notion of political Reason. The parameters or markers of this consciousness were absent from the figure of the subaltern, whose meaning making was independent from the elite's schematics of Reason and rationality. This absence did not mean an absent consciousness in the subaltern, but signified irreducible difference from the elite subject; in elite historiography, this difference was represented as absence. Here, the "thought of consciousness – and therefore of peasant subjecthood – as something immanent in the very practices of peasant insurgency" (Chakrabarty, 2000, p. 23) becomes crucial. In this construction of 'consciousness', it does not mean that consciousness existed inside the subaltern subject, or even that the subaltern subject was conscious of the full implications of his politics, but suggests that subaltern politics had a consciousness of its own, with logic that was not the same as that of elite consciousness. Subaltern consciousness, here, can be gauged as existing in the relationship between the subaltern and the elite – a relation that is always one of resistance on the part of the subaltern. In such a framework, the subaltern is constructed as autonomous insofar as he is constantly engaged in the reversal of signs – or symbols of authority – that hold him captive in a position of subordination with respect to the elite (Guha, 1983). This meant that subaltern consciousness could not be understood using the same parameters that mark elite consciousness; in fact, to use those markers to read subaltern consciousness would lead to the absence of any such consciousness, and a consequent blind spot in history where the subaltern figure was present.

This blind spot of history not only says something about the nature of the subaltern (and his consciousness), but also implicates the process of historiography and the larger field of politics from which the subaltern is absenced. Here, it is significant that the subaltern has been so far discussed within the context of the history of colonialism in India. During this time, the two predominant kinds of history writing – a colonialist version of history, written in order "to erect that past as a pedestal on which the triumphs and glories of the colonizers and their instrument, the colonial state, could be displayed to best advantage" (Guha, 1989, p. 211), and a bourgeois-nationalist history, whose motivation was "to represent Indian nationalism as primarily an idealist venture in which the indigenous elite led the people from subjugation to freedom" (Ibid., p. 2), had in common not only that they were both written from the vantage point of the elite, but also that both colluded in the project of colonization.

A consequence of this, for Guha, is that Indian nationalist historiography also gets caught within the paradigm of Western liberalism and its logic of capital, such that Indian nationalist history, insofar as it represented the elite bourgeoisie, produced an illusion of Western hegemony, an illusion that was created and maintained upon the erasure of subaltern consciousness in Indian history. Here, the specificity of Indian colonialism was in its manifestation of 'dominance without hegemony', where coercion on the part of the dominant and collaboration with this coercion on the part of the Indian bourgeoisie created conditions of subordination for the subaltern masses. It is within this bind of dominance and subordination that the subaltern is caught. This bind, insofar as it is linked here to an illusion of a hegemonic relationship that tends to displace the nature of the subaltern from Indian history, is also a contestation of cultural paradigms – between the interpretation of Indian history as replicating Western hegemony, and the specificity of dominance/subordination as a relation that explains Indian colonialism, the subaltern is placed as a figure of absence. For Guha (1989) "D[ominance]/S[ubordination] is a relation constituted by elements which derive their idioms from two very different paradigms of political culture . . . one of which is contemporary, British and liberal, and the other pre-colonial, Indian and semi-feudal" (p. 270). So, the figure of the subaltern would perhaps mark the grounds for a contestation of culture via historiography.

Towards sexual subaltern subjects 99

Further, the relation between dominance and subordination in relation to Indian colonial history is marked by Guha (1989) as such:

> what makes the relation of D[omination] and S[ubordination] *specific and adequate to the conditions of colonialism* is an ensemble of overdetermining effects constituted by what Lacan, in his interpretation of that key Freudian concept, has called 'a double meaning', with each political instance standing at the same time for 'a conflict long dead' and 'a present conflict' – that is, for that process of condensation and displacement by which the ideological moments of social contradictions in pre-colonial India and modern England were fused with those of the living contradictions of colonial rule to structure the relation D[omination]/S[ubordination] . . . there is nothing in our political culture of the colonial period that is not an outcome of this process of overdetermination. That outcome, in its phenomenal form, is a tissue of paradoxes . . . The element of the past, though dead, is not defunct. The contemporary element, so vigorous in its native metropolitan soil, finds it difficult to strike roots as a graft and remains shallow and restricted in its penetration of the new site. *The originality of our politics of the period lies precisely in such paradoxes* which pervade the entire spectrum of power relations.
>
> (p. 271)

In such a relation between dominance and subordination, between Western and Indian frames of reference, between a past that is present and a present that absents some*thing* of itself – the subaltern emerges as a figure that is not simply absented from historical accounts of Indian colonialism, but becomes a figure that, even when presented, or re-presented, is constructed as something other than itself. The subaltern in such historiography is systematically relegated to a realm outside the topology of politics, and is brought back into history as a figure without consciousness. In other words, the subaltern is made an object, and further, an object that is not the object of enquiry in historiography. This seems to be the very path Swapna and Sucheta's posthumous re-presentation has taken, where, caught between discourses that determine – and are determined by – queer politics in the Indian subcontinent and elsewhere, they are absent from their abstracted representation as objects who will further the agenda and reach of queer politics in India.

Considering such contestation that is grounded on the figure of the subaltern – between absence and re-construction, between cultural paradigms that mark Indian history – the task of the subaltern historian was of recovering the subaltern. In doing so, the subaltern and his history would be posited to critique – or provide a criticism of – the history of the dominant in India. This not only included the colonialist and nationalist versions of Indian history, but also took into its fold a history of India that was influenced by Marxist historical materialism (Chakrabarty, 2000). With respect to this tradition of history writing, Guha (1983) states:

> the radical historian is driven by the logic of his own incomprehension to attribute a deliberate falsehood to one of the greatest of our rebels . . . Blinded by the glare of a perfect and immaculate consciousness the historian sees nothing . . .
> *(pp. 37–40)*

The rebel is the subaltern, who is idealized as an abstract figure of the worker/peasant in these accounts of history, such that the abstraction takes away from the grounded nature of the subaltern. Further, this abstraction leads to a mediation of the subaltern's consciousness by the historian, who fails to recognize the many modalities of subaltern life, resistance, and political action, and even if recognition occurs, subaltern consciousness is interpreted as a not quite developed revolutionary consciousness (Prakash, 1994).

In light of all these versions of history that absented and re-presented the subaltern in their own ways, the task of the subaltern historian was even more difficult. The question to the subaltern historian had to do with how to reconfigure history to make the subaltern a subject of his own history, as opposed to the object in history that it had hitherto been. In light of this,

> [s]ubaltern historiography necessarily entailed (a) a relative separation of the history of power from any universalist histories of capital, (b) a critique of the nation-form, and (c) an interrogation of the relationship between power and knowledge (hence of the archive itself and of history as a form of knowledge).
> *(Chakrabarty, 2000, p. 15)*

Not only would this implicate history in the subject formation of the subaltern, but also seek to redefine what was considered politics, and what was left outside its field. In other words, the subaltern as subject would become the grounds for a larger reshaping of Indian history and politics, and would also provide cues towards newer understandings of power and its manifestations in Indian politics.

According to Guha (1983), historical texts could be categorized into primary, secondary, and tertiary documents, all of which were complicit in producing a code of 'counter-insurgency' to absent the subaltern subject. This process takes place as tertiary texts transform secondary ones – which were transformations of primary texts – and in this mutation, produce slippages, or "moments of risk" (p. 11) that produce meaning that is not necessarily implied by the text, but is inscribed to the text in that moment. Here, Guha attempts to break down the structure of language to determine the moments in which the text absents the subaltern subject, and mis-represents him as an object in history. As a result, history is determined by the "pattern of the historian's choice . . . [conforming] to a counter-code, the code of counter-insurgency" (Ibid., p. 19). It is a deliberate and repeated process through which the text goes against the insurgency of the subaltern, and as such, the subaltern historian must read the text against its grain to discover again the subaltern figure hiding there; "subalterns . . . do not disappear into discourse but appear in its interstices, subordinated by structures over which they exert pressure . . . [They] emerge between the folds of the discourse, in its silences and blindness, and in its overdetermined pronouncements" (Prakash, 1994, p. 1482). In other words, to read for the subaltern subject is to read against the text's absence and mis-re-presentations, perhaps to read against one's own desire, and discover again the figure of the subaltern, silent and persistent.

The gendered subaltern and the failure of re-presentation

It can be said that the subaltern figure was hitherto imagined primarily in terms of domination and subordination based on class. Instances of subaltern resistance did not seem to hold within their fold any gendered figures; it seems that women, insofar as they were demonstrative of gendered difference from men, were not considered central figures in subaltern studies. This absence of women from subaltern historiography was demonstrated by Spivak (1985), when she stated that "a feminist historian of the subaltern must raise the question of woman as a structural rather than marginal issue" (p. 361), possibly as an intervention that attempted to pull Subaltern Studies into a paradigmatic shift that would be inaugurated by presencing the figure of the woman into a theory of the subaltern that had previously focused on class as a category of analysis. The entry of the woman into subaltern studies would, for Spivak, imply a structural change in their approach to historiography and necessitate a redefinition of the subaltern, as opposed to the inclusion of women into the already established mode of history that was initiated through subaltern studies. This structural shift would not only mark the position of the woman differently, insofar as she was subaltern, but would shift the meaning of what it meant to be subaltern.

This argument was situated within a larger critique of the assumptions of subaltern theory regarding historiography and the subaltern as subject. For Spivak, the theorization of the subaltern subject was problematic because it approached the subaltern through an impression of consciousness as agency, and in the failure of the subaltern to demonstrate this agency, the subaltern historian finds himself repeatedly facing moments of failure in discovering 'subaltern consciousness':

> To investigate, discover, and establish a subaltern or peasant consciousness seems at first to be a positivistic project – a project which assumes that, if properly prosecuted, it will lead to firm ground, to some *thing* that can be disclosed. This is all the more significant in the case of recovering subaltern consciousness because . . . consciousness is *the* ground that makes all disclosures possible . . . even as 'consciousness' is thus entertained as an indivisible self-proximate signified or ground, there is a force at work here which would contradict such a metaphysics. For consciousness here is not consciousness-in-general, but a historicized political species thereof, subaltern consciousness.
>
> *(Ibid., p. 338)*

Here, it seems that Spivak is alerting the SSC to the predicament constituting subaltern consciousness as an always *present* thing to locate at the interstices of history, waiting to be found by the historian with the appropriate tools and the right gaze.

For Spivak, the SSC's assumption of subaltern agency as indivisible consciousness is problematic because it presupposes a central or undivided subaltern subject. This subject – in truth or as historical fact – is what the SSC will discover if their mode of historiography is correct or reflexive enough. Since no such subject seems to exist within Spivak's proposed framework, the subaltern historian is always met with failure when subaltern agency does not manifest itself in this manner. Prakash (1994) writes:

> [T]he subalternist search for a humanist subject-agent frequently ended up with the discovery of the failure of subaltern agency: the moment of rebellion always contained within it the moment of failure. The desire to recover the subaltern's autonomy was repeatedly frustrated because subalternity, by definition, signified the impossibility of autonomy.
>
> *(p. 1480)*

Here, failure seems to be attributed as a subject-effect of the subaltern, such that the subaltern is always doomed to a 'moment of failure', even in resistance. Spivak shifts the cause of this failure from the subaltern subject to the subaltern historian. In other words, for Spivak, the SSC presupposes a concrete subaltern subject as they undertake the task of presenting or re-presenting him in history to correct the injustice of his absenting in history; it is this very task of re-presentation of the subaltern that creates (or, perhaps repeats) its failure in history.

In such a reading of the Subaltern Studies project by Spivak, the role of failure in encountering the subaltern in history is linked to the 'continuous and homogenous' nature of subaltern consciousness. Such a consciousness posits the subaltern as "the effect of an effect ... or the substitution of an effect for a cause" (Spivak, 1985, p. 341). In other words, Spivak seems to be arguing against the subaltern as a material and discoverable subject, where this materiality not only imposes an effect on the subaltern that makes his subjectivity impossible to reach, but also brings a moment of failure to the subaltern historian in discovering the subaltern subject. This seems to be related to the approach of the SSC towards history, which Spivak categorizes as history seen through the registers of truth, fact, and presence. In such a mode of history writing, or such a methodology of historiography, the subaltern as end point of this process cannot help but be a concrete, deterministic, positivistic figure. For Spivak, since the subaltern is not such a subject, the subaltern historian also fails in his task of discovering the subaltern and placing him as a subject of his own history; this history is not the subaltern's own, but the one created by the subaltern historian, and possibly re-presents the subaltern as an object, albeit as an object different in nature from the subaltern object of elite historiography.

It seems that, for Spivak, the failure of discovering a subaltern figure is a problem that requires an epistemological and ontological restructuring of previously posited subaltern studies. She imagines another methodology for tracing the figure of the subaltern in its absence and presence in history which necessitates breaking away from disciplinary boundaries of history and literature, creating something that lies between fact and fiction (Spivak, 1987). If this methodology holds, the result might be a contingently presented subaltern figure, located at the interstices of disciplines, produced through different readings of the same text, or rather, brought to light through the contestations of meaning on the same grounds of production. This is what she attempts in a reading of '*Stanadayini*' by Mahasweta Devi, where she reads the story through many positions and demonstrates how the figure of the subaltern woman "is always the object of the gaze 'from above'" (Ibid., p. 129). In this reading, Spivak tries to read Jashoda as a subaltern woman who is posited as a figure that holds an excess of meaning; as if Jashoda carries the impossibility of being fully explained, or entirely interpreted. Aspects of Jashoda's existence fall within the frame of capital, gender, development, and race, but something always eludes meaning — Jashoda escapes full representation, even while being presented through contested meanings that explain her in part. With reference to how domination comes to determine the subaltern figure, Spivak states: "the relationship [between systems of domination and the subaltern] might not be 'dialectical' at all but discontinuous, 'interruptive'" (Ibid., p. 108).

This seems to be the nature of the (gendered) subaltern as Spivak understands it. It seems the subaltern, then, exists to demonstrate the limits of knowledge, only emerging through excess, interruption, and a crisis in disciplines. However, it is possible to read this limit or impossibility to fully theorize or represent the subaltern (woman) as a position devoid of its own agency, such that the subaltern figure is only demonstrative of irredeemable epistemic violence. In such a reading, "the colonized or Third World woman is, unlike the politically organized proletariat, paradigmatic of subalternity borne out of silencing, epistemic violence, and erasure. Her silencing marks the limits of what can be historically retrieved (subaltern voice) and epistemologically known (experience)" (Nilsen & Roy, 2015, pp. 8–9). It seems that this is the methodological trap that Spivak inaugurates in her own re-signification of the subaltern; in such a reading of Spivak, the subaltern subject is now as if outside politics and representation in an irremediable way, and as such, beyond agency and recovery.

However, another way of understanding Spivak's attempts to re-signify the subaltern is perhaps to read this process of arriving at the limits of meaning as one that demonstrates something about the nature of the epistemological presumptions that generate such limits. In other words, if the subaltern woman indeed eludes full representation, then it brings to light the biased grounds on which our knowledge systems are built. This is perhaps why Spivak sifts through numerous modes of knowledge production and places Jashoda at the limits of all of them – it demonstrates their complicity in the objectification of the subaltern through a 'gaze from above', while also saying something about the nature of the subaltern woman. If the subaltern is indeed placed at an epistemic void (in that she can never be fully recovered), then the way in which Spivak uses contending frames to develop contestations of meaning of that same void can only produce truths that lie between fact and fiction, unable to be read through registers of agency or consciousness. Then, for Spivak, the subaltern is at the "the *antre* [place of in-betweenness] of situational indeterminacy these careful historians presuppose as they grapple with the question, Can the subaltern speak?" (1988, p. 79).

It is with this question – of whether the subaltern can or cannot speak – that Spivak raises the issue of representation with respect to the subaltern. She differentiates between two kinds of representation, "representation as 'speaking for', as in politics, and representation as 're-presentation', as in art or philosophy" (Ibid., p. 70). The first can be seen as representation as proxy, where someone or something stands in for another, while the latter is representation as portrait, where someone re-presents or re-constructs another. It seems that the subaltern is trapped between these two kinds of representations, both of which co-opt her speech, made possible through epistemic violence that makes this co-option invisible, a forgetting of the forgotten that allows one to speak for – or represent – the subaltern, making her a homogenous object, as opposed to seeing her as a figure that is "irretrievably heterogeneous" (Ibid., p. 79). Spivak claims that the subaltern can "speak and know their conditions", given the possibility of political alliance and the right kind of infrastructure. But the subaltern also cannot speak, given the epistemic violence and (mis)re-presentation inherent in most intellectual and political thought. Simultaneously, the subaltern figure becomes the bearer of failure and possibility; the subaltern is imagined as a figure who can speak, in that her voice is being represented by proxy or portrait, as well as a subject who cannot speak, since this representation removes her from her own conditions. The subaltern, especially the subaltern woman, can therefore only be found in what "the work cannot say" (Ibid., p. 82), what lies in "the semiosis of the social text" (Ibid., p. 82).

Spivak uses the example of sati to demonstrate the position of the subaltern woman, such that sati becomes an event through which the Indian woman becomes grounds through which:

> white men, seeking to save brown women from brown men, impose upon those women a greater ideological constriction ... Between patriarchy and imperialism ... the figure of the woman disappears, not into a pristine nothingness, but into a violent shuttling which is the displaced figuration of the 'third-word woman' caught between tradition and modernization.
> *(Ibid., pp. 101–102)*

It is this phenomenon, through which the woman is constructed as an ideal wife to be saved from her own men under colonialism, that Sunder Rajan (2003) addresses when she claims that such a woman is neither placed as an object nor as a subject in her own history. This woman has a voice, but there is impossibility in speech; the act of defining oneself is barred. Further, even if the woman manages to speak, she will face a failure in comprehension. It is as if there is no discourse, no theory to which the woman can lay claim without being circumscribed by dominant discourse. Spivak juxtaposes this woman as ideal wife with an example of an unmarried young woman, Bhuvaneshwari Bhaduri, who hanged herself while menstruating to demonstrate that her death was not a result of an illicit pregnancy. It is this act of suicide that, for Spivak, becomes central in demonstrating the difficulty of the speech of the subaltern woman, who finds herself unable to speak within the registers into which she has been inscribed, and resorts to signification through an event like suicide. However, this suicide also holds a promise, it seems, in that it demonstrates the (im)possible space the subaltern woman comes to occupy to assert herself. In this assertion of the subaltern woman, co-option by dominant discourse will always leave an excess that will remain un-interpretable, and it is this excess that will be the moment in which the subaltern is discoverable.

II. Thinking through sexual subaltern subjects

I have taken this detour into a brief history of the subaltern figure inaugurated by the SSC only to highlight how much of its theorization may overlap with Swapna and Sucheta. Perhaps parallels can be drawn between how well-meaning historians were unable to discover the subaltern figure in its complexity and the way in which *Sappho for Equality* metonymized Swapna and Sucheta as one dimensional figures that represent the violence marking lesbian lives in India. In the previous chapter, I attempted to show how such representation also succeeds in objectifying and co-opting any radical difference Swapna and Sucheta may inhabit; in this failure to acknowledge their lives as *différance* (Derrida, 1968/1973), it is possible that we miss the opportunity to rethink the limits of queer politics and the discourses that frame it in Indian contexts.

Additionally, Spivak's intervention demonstrates that a resignification of a theory of the subaltern is possible, one that determines how newer subaltern figures emerge as social, economic, political, and cultural landscapes shift over time. Just as the SSC began to rethink the location and position of the subaltern figure in light of the liberalization of the Indian economy (Chakrabarty, 2000; Chatterjee, 2012), Spivak took the subaltern figure out of colonialism and located it in the framework of international division of labour as global economies became more porous across the West and the rest (Spivak, 1988). In doing so, Spivak highlighted how theoretical developments and political discourses were able to "conserve the subject of the West, or the West as Subject" (Ibid., p. 66). The gendered subaltern was perhaps imagined as a critique of the epistemic violence that was inherent in subscribing to a theory produced for and in the West and using it to describe non-West specificities and locations. Just as 'elite' paradigms were unable to locate the subaltern figure marked by class, and Western feminism was unable to portray the Third World woman as anything but destitute (Stephens, 1989), similarly, queer theory and politics also runs the very real risk of misrepresenting queer subjects who do not fit into their paradigmatic – and often Westward facing and cosmopolitan – definitions of queerness (Santiago, 2002).

On her part, Spivak has continued to think through and rewrite the answer to her question, 'can the subaltern speak?' In a talk she delivered in 2004, she spoke of the subaltern figure as "without access to lines of social mobility". Elsewhere, she wrote, "Subaltern is a position without identity . . . Subalternity is where social lines of mobility, being elsewhere, do not permit the formation of a recognizable basis of action . . . No one can say 'I am subaltern' in whatever language" (2005, pp. 475–476). Here, Spivak is talking of a figure that seems to be outside the nation-empire exchange in a way that it is and is not a citizen subject. The activities of the government and liberalization have penetrated their lives, but they do not have access to 'lines of social mobility' and cannot impact liberalization or the government in any way. In other words, such a figure may exist within the geographic borders of a nation-state but does not exist in its symbolic imaginations, nor in those of its citizen subjects (Butler & Spivak, 2010). They are technically citizens, but they do not seem to be subjects of the nation-state; the subaltern can be used for policy building, but is not in a position to impact or change policy (Spivak, 1993/2012). They cannot claim their own subaltern position, for the subaltern is fundamentally separated from any such articulation of identity. For Spivak, gender remains crucial to the subaltern figure, even though she now locates her in lower classes (Bhuvaneshwari Bhaduri was a middle-class woman), since the norm of reproductive heteronormativity is, for her, "the broadest and oldest global institution" (2005, p. 481).

In this framework, agency is seen as "institutionally validated action, assuming collectivity, distinguished from the formation of the subject, which exceeds the outlines of individual intention" (Spivak, 2005, p. 476), and as such, is far removed from the subaltern subject. Within these conditions, working with the subaltern, for Spivak, implies the creation of infrastructure with the subaltern that will allow her to speak in a register that will be recognized. Here, it seems that the task of learning from subalternity is to situate oneself at the margins of the empty space that exists between the subaltern and the nation-state; by doing so, agency can be brought close to the subaltern through synecdoche – "the part that seems to agree is taken to stand for the whole" (Ibid., p. 480). It is to metonymize oneself to claim a collectivity that eventually leads to agency. This is not the politics of representation as portrait or proxy, but a politics of collectivity where the subaltern researcher patiently learns from working with the subaltern, moving away from identity politics in the process.

However, it is unclear how such metonymization can occur, or how we can create infrastructure that bridges the gap across which the subaltern lives, especially if we situate the subaltern position as a void or aporia. Even if this process were possible, it is unsure whether it could be generalizable, since the conditions of possibility that enable the subaltern to speak for themselves include an attenuation to the specificity of their position. Over time, many have tried to think through the subaltern subject as a figure specific to a time and place, and "[f]rom its initial concentration in the history of nineteenth-century India, the temporal locus of Subaltern Studies has shifted forward in time, into contemporary society and politics" (Arnold, 2015, p. 258). Even though much criticism has established that the formulations of historiography and even concepts such as subaltern consciousness, or subalternity as representation, were deeply problematic, a case has been made that the questions asked by the SSC remain valid even today (Chatterjee, 2012; Chakrabarty, 2013; Arnold, 2015). It is perhaps the weight of those questions that has kept Subaltern Studies relevant to the contemporary, but it seems that current researchers of the subaltern must perhaps begin by answering why they think subaltern studies remains utilizable in their own fields, which are contextually and conceptually different from where subaltern studies first emerged. As Arnold (2015) writes, "any current reconceptualization of Subaltern Studies has to address the still pertinent question of what such a field of study is for" (p. 259), even if it retains the fundamental assumption that "the past could meaningfully be used to explain, interrogate, and structure the present" (Ibid., p. 259).

One such conceptualization of the subaltern in the contemporary is through the category of the 'sexual subaltern' perhaps first invoked by Kapur, in her work on sexual minorities in India, primarily in relation to the law (especially Article 377):[2]

> The term sexual subaltern is at one level intended to capture the extraordinary range and diversity of the counter-heteronormative movement . . . The subaltern subject is not simply a member of a minority group. While they are minorities in so far as they seek to claim formal equal rights, at a more radical level, this subject also brings about a conscious challenge to the dominant normative assumptions about the subject on which law is based. By virtue of her subaltern location and performance in a postcolonial space, the subaltern subject resists the assimilative gestures of the imperial and liberal project.
>
> *(Kapur, 2009, p. 385)*

Here, Kapur is trying to imagine a sexual subaltern subject on the grounds of their marginality and exclusion from the heteronorm. It is indeed possible to see a non-heterosexual or non-gender binary subject as being outside the 'institution' of reproductive heteronormativity and its exchange with the nation-state. It is also possible to locate this figure as one that embodies resistance, which was a central characteristic of the subaltern in its previous theorizations.

This sexual subaltern comes close to the conception of the sexual subaltern by Roy (2015), for whom "'subaltern' is employed both as an identitarian category and as a critical lens to study power: that is, to unearth the sites and workings of power" (p. 151). In Roy's use of the category of the 'sexual subaltern', like Kapur's definition, there are elements of being marginalized, and the potential for resistance that challenges not only sexuality and gender, but also cultural institutions like the family. For Roy, "[t]he idea of subalternity with respect to sexuality also potentially captures, to a greater extent than does 'queer', the relations and politics of subordination, exclusion, and invisibility attached to non-hegemonic sexual identities" (Ibid., p. 153). Here, the term 'subaltern', or 'subalternity', is deployed intersectionally, such that even if the sexual subaltern would be categorized as 'elite' in its previous usage, the claim to being a sexual subaltern subject still holds. Another term used to describe queer subjects as subaltern ones comes from Narrain and Gupta's (2011) analysis of the 'queer subaltern', whose voice has been absented in colonial history, and who is seen as a victim of larger processes of power. Consequently, it is their voicelessness that Narrain and Gupta attempt to recover through tracing a 'legal queer history'.

However, it seems that these readings of the sexual/queer subaltern do not adequately theorize sexuality or the subaltern figure, insofar as they do not make a case for why the term 'subaltern' is being attached to the category of the 'sexual', what encompasses the 'sexual' in this attachment, and what folds such attachment produces as a result. In other words, the consequences of inaugurating the category of the sexual subaltern seem unclear, even though the reason given to utilize this category is that it lays claim to a possibility of resistance in a subject who is marginalized. If it holds that the subaltern figure is one that is outside the nation-empire exchange, without the possibility of claiming its own subaltern position, and defined away from parameters of agency, consciousness, and therefore, what we conventionally understand as resistance, then the sexual subaltern figure invoked in such theorizations is not necessarily subaltern, most significantly because non-heterosexuality or queerness cannot become the only marker of marginality or a subaltern position.

In this deployment of the 'sexual subaltern', it is almost as if the subaltern becomes an empty category or referent for any marginality from which resistance can emerge; both readings by Kapur and Roy focus on these two aspects of the subaltern, or subalternity, without seeming to engage with other characteristics that determined the subaltern, like the question of subaltern consciousness and its objectification, its absence from history and its outsided-ness from the topology of political authorship and action, or even the question of an ethical mode of representing the subaltern in research, which is tied to the question of subaltern methodology. This same problematic can be seen in the deployment of the 'queer subaltern' by Narrain and Gupta (2011), who restrict the queer subaltern subject within the framework of law, where the reclamation of their voices would necessarily mean steps towards inclusive citizenship, and as such, erasure of difference.

Further, Nilsen and Roy (2015) define the subaltern through frames of agency and identity positions, contrary to the direction in which the subaltern was taken by the SSC or by Spivak in their work. They rethink subalternity as "(a) relational – that is, subalternity is above all a positionality . . . (b) intersectional – that is, subalternity is constituted along several axes . . . (c) dynamic – subalternity does not preclude agency" (Ibid., p. 12). The result of such redefinition is that "[s]ubalternity was thus conceptualized in relation to multiple social groups and the power relations between them. It was not reducible to any singular social axis – class or gender" (Ibid., p. 13). This shift is made to complicate "any quest for a 'pure' subaltern, circumventing problems of empirical classification of the 'real' subaltern" (Ibid., p. 14). However, it seems possible that a move to intersectionality in this context might be somewhat hasty, since it is not worked out as to how multiple axes of power or domination would come together to determine the figure of the subaltern in its context, or its specificity. Roy addresses this problem with respect to the sexual subaltern when she states, "some sexual subalterns are more subaltern than others in terms of their (in)ability to participate in political process and be intelligible" (Roy, 2015, p. 161). Perhaps the quantification of one form of subalternity as more or less than other forms of subalternity is a result of having rendered it a signifier that holds too many meanings. This theorization of the subaltern is perhaps a conflation of subalternity that exists in multiple forms, contexts, and locations with a specific subaltern position.

This question of the subaltern's position – as inside or outside discourse – seems to be one that cannot be escaped. Many critics of subaltern studies have pointed out that to put the subaltern figure absolutely outside discourse is to take away any possibility of resistance, voice, or agency from them. It is possible that these critiques might be emerging from a moment of slippage in subaltern studies itself, one that homogenizes the subaltern as position and subalternity as condition. This slippage, perhaps, makes it possible to debate the insided-ness or outsided-ness of the subaltern, such that the subaltern is positioned either inside or outside, but not as both. At this point, I think it might be important to consider a theoretical differentiation between 'subaltern' as position, 'subalternity' as condition, and 'subalternization' as process. Previous work on subaltern studies seems to make this distinction, although it is uncertain whether it has been clearly demarcated. From the trajectory of the 'subaltern', it is perhaps possible to state that the subaltern is a specific and material figure positioned outside the empire-nation exchange in a way that cuts off their lines of social mobility. Such a figure is the subaltern that the SSC tried to recover in colonial historiography, as well as the figure that cannot speak in any recognizable register according to Spivak. This figure, it seems, would still use their body as text, unable to speak in the language of the citizen of a nation-state.

In contrast, 'subalternity' could be theorized as a condition of exteriority, marginalization, oppression, and even epistemic violence at the hands of the dominant. In such an understanding, the subject would be categorized, or characterized, by their subalternity. Here, the difference lies in that this subject is not fully outside discourse (or even outside history or politics) in a way that makes them a non-citizen object of the nation-state; this subject – by virtue of their gender and/or sexuality, for example – would be outside one particular system of exchange, here, reproductive heteronormativity. However, a subject who was not subaltern, but possessed subalternity would remain a citizen subject. In other words, subalternity is demonstrative of being marginal on some axes, but is not a material position that circumscribes a subject and their body far from usual notions of social mobility, agency, or political action. 'Subalternization' would be the process by which a subaltern position, or subaltern condition, was being created within political or theoretical discourses, in a way that highlighting the process of subalternization would potentially bring to light the limits or biases of such discourses.

If this differentiation were to hold, then the shift to the sexual subaltern (as it has been made until now) would not be, perhaps, an adequate resignification of the subaltern but might come to depict a subject for whom their gender and/or sexuality is a cause of subalternity, as a condition of their existence. These subjects could be the possibly articulate subjects of queer politics, very much citizens of the nation-state, except when it comes to their gender and/or sexuality. These subjects would still be marginalized, and would still be demonstrative of the potential for radical political resistance, but their position would not be characterized as 'less subaltern' compared to subjects who were marginalized on more axes than theirs. At the risk of sounding facile, a poor gay Dalit man would not, within this framework that demarcates between subaltern and subalternity, be more subaltern than a middle-class upper caste lesbian. The subjects of Kapur's and Roy's work, then, would be subjects of sexual subalternity, but would not be sexual subalterns.

Swapna and Sucheta, on the other hand, could perhaps be sexual subaltern subjects, not only outside the exchange of reproductive heteronormativity, outside the exchange between empire and nation, on the other side of power in the international division of labour, but also outside discourses of queerness and sexuality that characterize contemporary queer politics in India. We have seen how Swapna's and Sucheta's subjectivities are different from the subjects who author queer politics, and their voices cannot be found in the fragmented field of queer politics in India. In fact, it might even be that readings of their death – by authors of queer politics, and otherwise – have represented them much like the subaltern was represented in colonial or nationalist history (or perhaps by subaltern studies before Spivak's intervention), such that they were present, but as mis-representations, essentially absent from their own documentations.

At least two things seem to be important for a discussion on Swapna and Sucheta as sexual subaltern subjects. First, that they have been hitherto present as absence in their representations, which reveals the nature of power that works not only on the side of the reproductive heteronorm, but even on its other side. If Swapna and Sucheta can indeed be seen as sexual subaltern subjects, with a position outside the discourses that have sought to represent them, then they can turn back upon those very discourses to reveal their limits, their centres, and their margins. It is possible that Swapna and Sucheta can demonstrate the circuits of power that operate in the discursive productions of queer politics in India, as well as highlight its complicities. Further, if we see Swapna and Sucheta as occupying radical difference not only from reproductive heterosexuality, but also its seemingly Other – queer politics, then would we imagine them to be the Other of queer politics, haunting its discourses from within?

This position of radical difference, something that the SSC claimed would only be understood when we resignified – or at least expanded – the fields of politics and history itself, is also the claim of resistance without power in Samaddar's logic of the political subject. Both take us towards a language of political resistance that cannot be co-opted by those it opposes; there is a fundamental incommensurability of this resistance to the language of those on the side of power. It requires a shift in what we have hitherto thought of as queer politics; the sexual subaltern subject cannot be included into its already existing structures, cannot be understood in the many queer tongues such politics speaks. If a moment of inclusion did occur, the sexual subaltern subject would perhaps no longer be a subaltern subject. The very criterion of the sexual subaltern position is that it lies away from the discourses that operate with the logic of inclusion, for it is inclusion that also excludes, and excludes them specifically as sexual subaltern subjects. Further, such a conceptualization would move away from the logic of human rights and legal reform, both of which are driven towards an individual sense of the subject, and an equalization of difference. The sexual subaltern subject can perhaps not be understood within the logic of individualism, even while collectivization must possibly be worked towards, not already having been pre-given as a condition of such a subject.

Finally, the sexual subaltern subject is in a position to shift not only the field of queer politics, but the meaning of queerness itself. It can imbricate the symptoms of queer politics, and reveal something of its drives and desires, demonstrating the limits of knowledge structures that produce queer discourses. As such, it may provide a way to resignify queerness at the level of the symbolic, and reach a politics that is attuned to a subject who is radically different without reducing, misrepresenting, or including that *differance* within its folds.

III. Interlude

If Swapna and Sucheta cannot be represented as sexual subaltern subjects, it may not only be a question of disciplines and knowledge, but also of methodology. How would we study a sexual subaltern subject? Where and how would we locate their subjectivity and speech? If we do not have a knowledge that is not violent to them, we also do not have an existing methodology that does not always already absent them . . . What does a sexual subaltern subject need from the researcher? How should a researcher approach such a subject, with what orientations, with which gaze? How could a researcher attend to the field in which the sexual subaltern can first be found, in their absent-presence, while also attending to the simultaneous materiality of their lives, which perhaps seem metaphysical in most frames of reference? How could a researcher remain ethical and responsible, without even knowing who they are, and what it means to be in their position? How could a researcher relate, but not co-opt? Perhaps it requires not only a breaking of disciplines, but also of methods . . .

Notes

1   In this chapter, I shift from 'he' to 'she' as the default gender of the subaltern figure in line with the SSC's imagination of such a figure.
2   The 'sexual subaltern', as invoked in this instance and this book, is markedly different from the invocations of 'subaltern sexuality' (for example, as deployed by Pandit (2013) where she writes on 'gendered sexual subalternity'). The difference lies in how the 'sexual subaltern' is used to discuss non-heterosexuality in tandem with subaltern/ity in this work, whereas 'subaltern sexuality' is not necessarily non-heterosexual, or rather, is almost always heterosexual in most usages of the term. Both terms are related to gender or gendered representation, albeit in different ways; the sexual subaltern relates to gender through non-heterosexual paths, and vice versa, whereas subaltern sexuality relates to gender through heterosexuality.

> . . . *They have forcibly gotten her married to some boy, who has not truly accepted her/whom she has not truly accepted. They have gotten her married, causing her a lot of pain, telling her horrible things about me, after having called people and insulted me and my family in front of everyone. Day after day they have tortured me. Day after day they continue to torture me, that no human being is capable of tolerating. Even after getting her married, to this day they have not let me be in peace. They beat her up and got her married. After that, where they got her married, there they used to torture her, and blame me for it. Even if we have not spoken to each other, they say we have spoken to each other. We haven't seen each other . . . talking to each other comes later, we have not even managed to glance at each other. Even then, they are suspicious of us. Now you only tell me, why will anyone tolerate this? It is better to die. Nobody from my family is responsible for my death. The ones who are responsible are those who have tortured me, those who have not let me live in peace. Do not forgive them ever, never. Everyone in my family likes-loves me a lot. There is no blame on them. I hope no harm will come to them. Please forgive me Ma, Baba, for causing you pain. I cannot live without my like-love. Please all of you stay well, stay at peace. Do not destroy any of my things. Do not look for me. I will not come back. Brothers, please care for Baba and Ma. Do not cause them any hurt ever. Take care of my elder sisters. Please do not be angry with me. I am not angry with you. I am telling the truth. Do not look for me. Please all of you stay well. Look at the book in Ma's name, do not give her any trouble. If the two of us die together, keep us together in one place, wherever that is. And if we stay alive, we will go far away . . . far away . . . and will not come back. I am repeating, my family is not to blame. There is some pending money to be collected for tuitions – from the elder wife, 200 rupees; Papai, 20; Jayan, 40; Pintu, 60; Pama, 70. All the money is under the mattress, take it.*
>
> Swapna's letter, page 5.
Translation mine[1]

Note

1 In the translation, I have used the phrase 'like-love' for the Bengali phrase *'bhalo basha'* or *'bhalo laga'*. I have done so for the following reasons: first, I would like to maintain the ambivalence of translating the sentiment of *'bhalo basha'* or *'bhalo laga'* into English, since it is a sentiment that is used to describe friendship and/or love in Bengali. Second, the ambivalence renders uncertain the nature of Swapna and Sucheta's relationship – were they lovers? Were they friends? Were they companions or partners of another kind? Finally, the phrase 'like-love', hyphenated as it is, suggests – for me – the limits and the promise of translation in the same moment.

6
MELANCHOLY, UNCERTAINTY, RESPONSIBILITY

> As always, death, which is neither a present to come nor a present past, shapes the interior of speech, as its trace, its reserve, its interior and exterior difference: as its supplement.
>
> *(Derrida, 1976/2002, p. 315)*

In the many detours this work has taken and throughout the arguments it has put forth, I have tried to keep Swapna and Sucheta alive. This has always already been a failed project, because no words can bring them to life, and there do not seem to be any knowledge systems or political infrastructures in place that can tell their story without misrepresenting them. And yet, this work has also been a necessary one, for in its detours and dead-ends, it is a reminder of the limits of the politics, theoretical disciplines, and discourses on which we rely to make queer lives more inhabitable. Swapna and Sucheta, to a large extent, are remainders of what queer politics has emerged from, the grounds it currently stands on, and the futures it intends to build. In turn, queer politics, its utopias, and its imaginations are not insular and are part of a larger matrix of epistemologies and their histories. As such, queer politics inherits from other discourses lessons in solidarity building as well as differentiations along the lines of gender, body, economy, race, caste, and geography that often tie together in the same moment the claiming of a queer identity with the un-naming of other positions.

In India, as well as across the world, queer politics is imperfect, segregated, and exclusionary. In the fragments of queer politics that I have tried to stitch together in this book, these segregations demonstrate how varied the voices of queer politics in India can be. At the same time, a somewhat stable imagination of the Hindu nationalist, upper-class, globalized queer can be seen peeking through almost unanimous demands of queer politics to seek inclusive citizenship and assimilation into the nation-state. To reach an assertion of queerness, especially in a country where non-heterosexuality is still illegal, has its own journey fraught with marginality and a violent becoming which cannot be undermined. At the same time, the processes behind who is able to inhabit queerness and to what extent in an increasingly cosmopolitan India also need urgent examination. In current political climates, where the promise of globalization and protection of nationalism are coming together to determine which subjects benefit from the illusion of 'free' markets and accrue cultural capital, and at what costs, queer subjects are being positioned in opposition to each other. Queer politics across the globe already warns us about the exclusions produced within queer spaces that relegate some queers from within its midst to disavowed or abject spaces that lie between memory and history, and there is an emergent danger of producing cultures and kinships of queerness premised on the collective forgetting of such queer figures. Over and over, we have realized that queer identity cannot be the only grounds on which we build our solidarities. As such, this book is a way to document queer politics in India by keeping the uneasy memory of Swapna and Sucheta in a position that puts the radical potential of queer identity politics under erasure.

To try and locate Swapna and Sucheta's place with respect to queer politics in India, this book has insistently moved in two apposite directions, trying to make meaning of the dialectic between contemporary queer politics and its subjects, between queer political subjects and sexual subaltern subjects, between 'global' directions of queer politics and 'local' articulations of queer sexuality, and between imaginations of subjectivity in politics and psychoanalysis. In doing so, I hope there is a disruption in the linearity and certainty of what gets constructed as truth and what is relegated to fiction. What queer politics takes to be the truth of 'queerness' or the 'queer subject' also determines what is considered meaningful and what can be resignified in queer political futures, because "[i]n concerning itself with what constitutes as truth, the field of discourse is also the field of political possibility" (Judge, 2018, p. 5). As such, I try to demonstrate how Swapna and Sucheta's metonymization by queer politics is necessarily violent and riddled with erasure and forgetting because the processes, discourses, and structures that determine the truth of queerness work against them, their modes of meaning making, and their subjectivities as sexual subaltern subjects. Their repudiated place at the outside of most discourses that determine queer politics in India today also forecloses possibilities of re-imagining sexuality beyond the reductive, and often Western, tropes of identity and sexual behaviour.

To reach a conceptualization of Swapna and Sucheta as sexual subaltern subjects is, in many ways, a bold claim, and requires more sustained work. At this juncture, it highlights the conditions to which they are subjected by mainstream structures of reproductive heterosexuality and by the marginal centres of power that become the benchmarks of queer politics and, consequently, decide meanings of queerness. To think of Swapna and Sucheta as sexual subaltern subjects is also to be attuned to their position in a topology of queer politics that can perhaps help us to see the disaggregated ways in which various queer subjectivities are centrally or obliquely placed in relation to heterosexual and queer worlds. Not all queer bodies are marked the same, and not all queer words are heard. And yet, this book also aims to serve as a reminder of their return. To think of Swapna and Sucheta as sexual subaltern subjects is to be attuned to their ability to not only demonstrate the limits of disciplines and discourses that try to rewrite the truth of their lives, but also to inhabit these structures of signification and power as traces of what they have put outside their boundaries, put outside their memories.

On methodology

To think of Swapna and Sucheta as sexual subaltern subjects is also to grapple with the question of method, because the subaltern subject constantly puts existing knowledges and disciplines to crisis. For sexual subaltern subjects, knowledge and truth do not overlap, but rather, exist as contention. In their case:

> Whatever the political necessity for holding the position, and whatever the advisability of attempting to 'identify' (with) the other as subject in order to know her, knowledge is made possible and is sustained by irreducible difference, not identity. What is known is always in excess of knowledge. Knowledge is never adequate to its object.
>
> *(Spivak, 1987, p. 112)*

As such, there seems to be a gap between knowledge and its object, and it is within this gap that there is space to manoeuvre away from or between disciplines, to deconstruct how knowledges are produced. If this work must remain faithful to Swapna and Sucheta as sexual subaltern subjects, then it cannot claim to be on the side of disciplinary knowledges or political theories that have hitherto failed to represent such subjects. This subject, with its own modes of being, and its own logic of mobility and solidarity, requires from the reflexive and ethical researcher a fundamental irreverence towards such systems of knowledge production, and an undisciplined and critical approach towards a politics that defends its borders with violence in the name of marginality and identity.

Throughout this book, I have attempted to shift from and sift through various disciplines – feminism, queer theory, Lacanian psychoanalysis, subaltern studies, cultural studies – in the hope that somewhere from within the folds of these disciplines and their political histories, I will be able to provisionally position Swapna and Sucheta as that material and transcendental non-thing that, having been outsided from and *object*ed (to) by all these knowledges, turns back upon them, never having left, or having left (as) a *trace*. Within a Derridean framework, the trace is the presence of an absence, an absence that may often be an exclusion, an absence that haunts the structure, that tracks its own trajectory within the structure, forever threatening to destabilize it from within, with a perspective of without (Derrida, 1976/2002; 1967/1978). Like the sexual subaltern subject, a trace has an ontological logic that differs from the structure in which it tracks its circuit, and as such, has its own language of signification. Insofar as Swapna and Sucheta are queer subaltern subjects, they can be seen operating with an ontologically different logic than the systems of signification that determine the discourses of queer politics in India.

In order to think of a subject who has a subjectivity that works as a supplement within discourses and disciplines, leaving a trace that brings us to the limits of understanding and language, it seemed no one method, rooted in any particular discipline, would be enough. This work, then, can at best claim that what it presents, and the journey it takes, is marked by an effort at bricolage, a piecing together of interdisciplinary tools to expose and understand what lies at its margins or limits – the sexual subaltern figure. Here, bricolage is the only way of understanding an epistemic and metaphysical field, for knowledge can never "coincide with its "means" (Spivak, 1976/2002, p. xix). This implies that the field is never entirely knowable, and the myth of knowingness is what can then be deconstructed through bricolage, such that knowledge is no longer possessed or definitive, but is now subject to the play of significations, to difference and *différance*, to the metaphysics of presence and absence, to the work of the trace.

What is produced because of bricolage is not a knowledge of certainty, but perhaps a knowledge that builds itself from an inherent gap that I am calling here the work of division; starting from the research question that took this project in two directions – locating Swapna and Sucheta amid layers of representation, and mapping queer politics in India – to the duality that marks the very nature of this writing. What is written in this book is not entirely definitive, but it is also not entirely fictive – it can be seen as divided (or conjoined) between fact and fiction. It represents a kind of reality outside authenticity or inauthenticity, that is both true and false, complete and incomplete in what it represents.

And yet, perhaps for the sexual subaltern subject, even a methodology that is made amenable to bricolage is not enough. The bricoleur (the person who undertakes the task of bricolage) takes what tools they have at hand and uses them to construct and deconstruct the object or subject in question; as queer feminists theorizing on sexual subaltern subjects, we need to *make* these tools and create new theories and politics that we can inhabit, instead of trying to fit pieces of sexual subaltern subjects in multiple disciplines, however irreverently. To try and follow the trace of the sexual subaltern subject across contexts therefore seemingly entails building new infrastructure and new ways of seeing, probably at the cost of making the boundaries of disciplines and politics more porous.

As such, this methodology is in its initial stages, for to bring two methods together is also to cleave disciplines and knowledges that have different structural logics, and requires the task of translation in order for them to co-exist with each other. At the same time, the critique that such a patchwork methodology entails, particularly in the context of this work, is also a difficult one to arrive at. What I have written in this book comes in equal parts from my own engagement with queer and queer feminist spaces for the past few years, from texts that have emerged from within and outside queer movements in India, from conversations with friends, comrades, and allies who have tried to walk alongside me in my journey to ask and answer questions, and from my own history of moving from mainstream psychology to critical psychology, cultural studies, critical theory, and feminist and queer theories. As such, any critique that implicates these disciplines and these politics also imbricates me, exposes my fault-lines and failures. This work is not only divided between Swapna and Sucheta on one side, and the knowledges and politics that have failed them, but the work of division and dialectic is also visible in the way in which Swapna and Sucheta are at a distance from my own subjectivity as a researcher. As such, even as this book is ending, the work is only beginning, for this distance is yet to be traversed, or at least, made sense of in ways that can construct something beyond critique.

Between melancholy and responsibility

Perhaps it is possible that the division and dialectic that have characterized this work can be considered not only the result of interdisciplinarity, but also a consistent work of gender and sexuality itself. Butler returns to Freud's conceptualization of melancholia and assimilates it into the psychoanalytic structuration of gender and sexuality in a way that makes loss and refused identification of desire central to the stability of heterosexual orientations. She analyses the Freudian bodily ego as the seat of gender, where it is characterized by "the sedimentation of objects loved and lost, the archaeological remainder, as it were, of unresolved grief" (Butler, 1997, p. 133). Melancholia is seen as a necessary process in order to let the lost object go, the price of which is an incorporation of the lost object within the bodily (gendered) ego such that the lost object becomes a part of the subject through identification, which becomes "a psychic form of preserving the object" (Ibid., p. 134). Here, "letting the object go means, paradoxically, not full abandonment of the object but transferring the status of the object from external to internal" (Ibid., p. 134). This is what Butler refers to as a melancholic incorporation, where melancholia continues by disavowing the loss, delaying it such that the incorporation continues and the recognition of loss is postponed.

For Butler, a heterosexual culture demands the loss of same-sex attachments, while also demanding that such losses not be grieved. These demands come together to foreclose the possibility of homosexual or queer futures, which come to be characterized by "unlivable passion and ungrievable loss" (Ibid., p. 135). She claims that the fundamental psychoanalytic and anthropological Law – the taboo on incest – itself presupposes heterosexuality. Before the Law, therefore, lie foreclosed homosexual or queer possibilities. As such, heterosexuality is not the natural order of things, but an achievement that hinges on melancholic gender identifications. According to Freud's understanding of oedipality, for the

Melancholy, uncertainty, responsibility   125

girl to become successfully heterosexual, she must disavow her attachment to her mother in a way that forecloses all future same-sex attachments, finally finding solace in identifying with the mother. The boy, in this logic, must repudiate the feminine and its natural counterpart – desire for the masculine. He finds consolation in the wanting of what he could not identify with, and his orientation is now geared towards heterosexuality. For Butler, at both sites of oedipal resolution lies an uneasy disavowal of queer desires. Since queer desires lie at the very heart of heterosexuality like a trace, its maintenance requires not only a disavowal of queerness, but also a refusal to mourn its losses.

Within this framework, gender "itself might be understood in part as the "acting out" of unresolved grief" (Ibid., p. 146). Gender then becomes a symptom of the disavowal of queer desires, and as its foreclosed Other, queerness lies at the very heart of the structural melancholy of gender as the ungrievable object that constantly reminds heterosexuality of its frailty. When queer lives express themselves in a rejection of heterosexuality that follows the same process of exclusion by virtue of which heterosexuality others queer desires, then they not only "attribute a false and monolithic status to heterosexuality" (Ibid., p. 148), but also miss the opportunity to "work on the weakness in heterosexual subjectivation and to refute the logic of mutual exclusion by which heterosexism proceeds" (Ibid., p. 148). Queer lives, and queer politics, therefore, are not necessarily engaged in the act of *queering*, if we understand queering to be a politically subversive response or site of radical difference (or *différance*) that cracks dominant structures of oppression. Here, Butler suggests that perhaps "only the decentered subject is available to desire" (Ibid., p. 149) in a way that moves away from the melancholy and prohibitive logic of heterosexuality. Perhaps this decentred subject position, like the sexual subaltern subject, like the trace, can become grounds for a new language of resistance that is attuned to desire in a way that cannot be co-opted by the structures against whose grain desire operates in the first place.

In extending this framework of melancholic incorporation to this research, perhaps I can attribute the work of division to my own incorporation of Swapna and Sucheta as the ungrievable Other I have lost but cannot mourn. I had learned of their deaths in 2012, and my own hesitant and always questioning forays into queer politics began soon afterwards. Perhaps because I was always in part affected by the function of Swapna and Sucheta's memory, the organizations and collectives I eventually began to associate with and become a part of were simultaneously highly rewarding spaces for me while also being spaces that kept Swapna and Sucheta's question alive. I, too, was divided between the failures of queer politics and the promise it somehow always managed to carry. This research, then, could be seen as an exercise towards resolving the melancholy process of their persistent memory in how I live my every day. Perhaps to be menaced by this melancholy is productive in that it keeps the divide between Swapna and Sucheta and me alive, however paradoxically.

To think of Swapna and Sucheta as the remainder of my own politics (with its own logic of materiality, linearity, and temporality that does not necessarily match their present-absence) is to remain ambivalent in my own centred subject position/s, caught between my own words, agency, motivations, and the haunting question that is the twisted message of the Other, such that Swapna and Sucheta always put me to question, threatening my certainty by placing it under erasure so that *I* remain slightly displaced but necessarily there at the same time. Not unlike the Lacanian schema of the subject, between me and Swapna and Sucheta there is a relation to knowledge that is not linear, singular, and remains incomplete; this also marks the nature of writing in this text. As such, the sexual subaltern subject can perhaps help reveal the truth of the queer political subject, waiting to be found from the interstices of the intersubjective text that carries the mark of an encounter between these two subjects.

This ambivalence, the uneasy incorporated dialectic between me and Swapna and Sucheta is a characteristic feature of Freud's conception of melancholia (Freud, 1917/2006), and can perhaps be helpful in highlighting the role of the researcher insofar as their enquiry is hinged on a sexual subaltern subject. Insofar as it is possible to appropriate and define the characteristics of the subaltern subject, ossify the boundaries of subalternity, and decide the meanings of authentic subaltern subjectivity, then we must take the question of becoming a well-intentioned vanguard of the subaltern figure seriously. Queer politics in India can be seen as an example of how well-intentioned politics also sometimes fails to represent the subaltern figure, for it is exactly its intentions that produces a blind spot in its desire to re-present the subaltern. The real challenge of the subaltern, here the sexual subaltern, is that it can shed light on the limits of one's own politics; the sexual subaltern is in a position to make one fold back on one's own theoretical and political positions, for the sexual subaltern figure, just like the gendered subaltern figure, lies outside its structural margins.

The ambivalence of a melancholy relation with the sexual subaltern, then, can be the ambivalence of choosing between one's own well-intentioned theoretical-political standpoints or cultivating a patient work on the political and psychoanalytic self, as well as a work on one's given methodological tools, in order to begin to build a bridge between oneself and the sexual subaltern. The task of translation between researcher and researched in this instance relies on, according to Spivak (2004), the creation of infrastructure that allows the subaltern to represent themselves, a process that cannot be undertaken without working *with* the subaltern, during which the researcher metonymizes oneself. At the same time, if Butler's theorization of melancholy gender is to be believed, then what it demonstrates to us is the immense cost of not only heterosexuality, but of queerness as well; within this frame, to be queer is to remain trapped within a dialectic of love and loss. In a politics that grapples with that cost in its own ways, the urgency and helplessness in the face of a suicide like Swapna and Sucheta's cannot be underscored enough. There seems to be a price to be paid for hesitation, the least of which would mean that one needs to remain with one's hesitations and uncertainties in a structure of politics that almost seems to demand certain, sure truths. However, perhaps the price of not remaining with one's uncertainties is also rather great, for it fails to represent the sexual subaltern subject.

As such, to work towards hearing the speech of the sexual subaltern subject without translation, in its own system of signification and reference, is to also work towards a different logic of what currently constitutes not only queerness, but sexuality itself. It is to perhaps attempt to change the referent of queer politics from heterosexuality to something else, to shift the very language of sexuality. Insofar as language determines subjectivity, and is written and writes the body, this is to rethink sexuality in relation to the body, of thinking through the skin and the psyche. Insofar as the language of sexuality is also a discourse that undergoes its own becoming within political, cultural, and social contexts, to rethink the language of sexuality is to reimagine their boundaries. And yet, to reinvent a new language of sexuality is, in many ways, to shed our very skins and create newer ways to live our lives and orient ourselves to the world; is the trace of the sexual subaltern subject strong enough for us to reimagine our politics, rethink our queerness? Do we grieve them enough, does their absence make itself present in our everyday enough?

Perhaps, then, to feel responsibility towards Swapna, Sucheta, and other sexual subaltern subjects; to be grieved at their loss and silence is to feel the urgent need to build different frameworks that create conditions for their speech. This might mean shifting from an identity politics to a politics of identification, such that Swapna and Sucheta become the remainders of a grief we have not yet come to articulate; Swapna and Sucheta can be the reminders of a political-theoretical task we are yet to undertake, a task that builds a bridge between queer politics and sexual subaltern subjects.

BIBLIOGRAPHY

Achuthan, A. (2001) 'Development, difference, incommensurability, and the (im)possibilities of universalism'. In *From the Margins* Vol. I, No. II.
Agnes, F. (2002) 'Law, Ideology and Female Sexuality: Gender Neutrality in Rape Law'. In *Economic and Political Weekly*, March.
Agnes, F. (2008) 'Family Courts: From the Frying Pan into the Fire?'. In *Women's Studies in India: A Reader* (Ed. Mary E. John). New Delhi: Penguin.
Ahmed, S. (2006) 'Orientations: Towards a Queer Phenomenology'. In *GLQ: A Journal of Lesbian and Gay Studies* 12:4.
Ahmed, S. (2017) *Living a Feminist Life*. Durham: Duke University Press.
Ailawadi, D. (2014) 'Legislating (lesbian) Sexuality: Colonial Law and Post-Colonial Impact'. In *Annual Review of Critical Psychology* 11.
Altman, D. (1997). 'Global Gaze/Global Gays'. In *GLQ: A Journal of Lesbian and Gay Studies* 3:4.
Altman, D. (2001) 'Rupture or Continuity: The internationalization of gay identities'. In *Postcolonial, Queer: Theoretical Intersections* (Ed. John C. Hawley). New York: SUNY Press.
Anthias, F. (2013) 'Identity and Belonging: conceptualizations and political framings'. Working Paper No. 8. KLA Working Paper Series.
Arendt, H. (2005) *The Promise of Politics* (Ed. Jerome Kohn). New York: Schocken Books.
Arnold, D. (2015) 'Subaltern Studies: Then and Now'. In *New Subaltern Studies: Reconceptualizing Hegemony and Resistance in Contemporary India* (Eds. Alf Gunvald Nilsen & Srila Roy). New Delhi: Oxford University Press.
Bacchetta, P. (2007) 'Rescaling Transnational "Queerdom": Lesbian and "Lesbian" Identitary-Positionalities in Delhi in the 1980s'. In *Sexualities* (Ed. Nivedita Menon). New Delhi: Kali for Women.

Bandyopadhyay, S. (2012) 'Approaching the "Present": A Pre-Text – The *Fire* Controversy'. In *Sibaji Bandyopadhyay Reader: An Anthology of Essays*. Kolkata: Worldview.
Basu, A.R. (2006) *Lesbianism in Kolkata*. Kolkata: *Sappho for Equality*.
Beauvoir, S. (1949/2011) *The Second Sex*. London: Vintage.
Bose B. (2007) 'The Desiring Subject: Female Pleasures and Feminist Resistance in Deepa Mehta's *Fire*'. In *The Phobic and the Erotic: The Politics of Sexualities in Contemporary India* (Eds. Brinda Bose & Shubhabrata Bhattacharyya). Calcutta: Seagull.
Bose, B. & Bhattacharyya, S. (2007) 'Introduction'. In *The Phobic and the Erotic: The Politics of Sexualities in Contemporary India* (Eds. Brinda Bose & Shubhabrata Bhattacharyya). Calcutta: Seagull.
Brown, W. (2004). '"The Most We Can Hope For . . .": Human Rights and the Politics of Fatalism'. In *The South Atlantic Quarterly*, 103:2.
Butler, J. (1990) *Gender Trouble: Feminism and the Subversion of Identity*. New York: Routledge.
Butler, J. (1997) 'Subjection, Resistance, Resignification: Between Freud and Foucault' and 'Melancholy Gender/Refused Identification'. In *The Psychic Life of Power: Theories in Subjection*. California: Stanford University Press.
Butler, J. & Spivak, G.C. (2010) *Who Sings the Nation-State?* Calcutta: Seagull.
Campaign for Lesbian Rights (*Caleri*) (1999) *Lesbian Emergence: A Citizen's Report*. New Delhi: *Campaign for Lesbian Rights*.
Carastathis, A. (2013) 'Identity Categories as Potential Coalitions'. In *Signs* 38:4, Intersectionality: Theorizing Power, Empowering Theory.
Chakrabarty, D. (2000) '*Subaltern Studies* and Postcolonial Historiography'. In *Nepantla: Views from the South* 1:1
Chakrabarty, D. (2013) 'Subaltern Studies in Retrospect and Reminiscence'. In *Economic and Political Weekly* Vol. XLVIII, No. 12.
Chakravarti, P. (2010) 'Reading Women's Protest in Manipur: A Different Voice?'. In *Journal of Peacebuilding and Development* 5:3.
Chatterjee, P. (2012) 'After Subaltern Studies'. In *Economic and Political Weekly* Vol. XLVII, No. 35.
Chaudhury, A., Das, D., & Chakrabarti, A. (2000) 'Preface'. In *Margin of Margin: Profile of an Unrepentant Postcolonial Collaborator*. Collaborator: Anushtup.
Chen, M. (2012) *Animacies: Biopolitics, Racial Mattering, and Queer Affect*. Durham: Duke University Press.
Chesler, P. (2005) *Women and Madness*. New York: Palgrave Macmillan.
Chiesa, L. (2007) 'The Subject of the Imaginary (Other)' and 'The Unconscious Structured Like a Language'. In *Subjectivity and Otherness: A Philosophical Reading of Lacan*. Massachusetts: The MIT Press.
Chow, R. (2001) 'Gender and Representation'. In *Feminist Consequences: Theory for the New Century* (Eds. Elisabeth Bronfen & Misha Kavka). New York: Columbia University Press.
Cohen, L. (2005) 'The Kothi Wars: AIDS Cosmopolitanism and the Morality of Classification'. In *Sex in Development: Science, Sexuality, and Morality in Global*

Perspective (Eds. Vincanne Adams & Stacy L. Pigg). Durham: Duke University Press.

Copjec, J. (1994) *Read My Desire: Lacan against the Historicists*. Massachusetts: MIT Press.

Cuellar, D. P. (2010) 'The Symbolic and the Imaginary', 'The Signifier and the Signified', and 'The Representative of the Subject'. In *From the Conscious Interior to an Exterior Unconscious: Lacan, Discourse Analysis and Social Psychology* (Eds. Danielle Carlo & Ian Parker). London: Karnac.

Darwish, M. (2009) 'From now on you're somebody else'. In *A River Dies of Thirst* (Trans. Catherine Cobham). London: Saqi.

Davar, B. (1999) *Mental Health of Indian Women: A Feminist Agenda*. New Delhi: Sage.

Dave, N. (2012) *Queer Activism in India: A Story in the Anthropology of Ethics*. Durham: Duke University Press.

Davidson, A. (2001) *The Emergence of Sexuality: Historical Epistemology and the Formation of Concepts*. Massachusetts: Harvard University Press.

Derrida, J. (1968/1973) 'Differance'. In *Speech and Phenomena and Other Essays on Husserl's Theory of Signs* (Trans. David Allison). USA: Northwestern University Press.

Derrida, J. (1967/1978) 'Structure, Sign, and Play in the Discourse of the Human Sciences'. In *Writing and Difference* (Trans. Alan Bass). London: Routledge.

Derrida, J. (1993) *Aporias* (Trans. Thomas Dupoit). California: Stanford University Press.

Derrida, J. (2002) 'Force of Law: The "Mystical Foundation of Authority"'. In *Acts of Religion* (Trans. Gil Anidjar). New York: Routledge.

Derrida, J. (1976/2002) *Of Grammatology* (Trans. Gayatri Spivak). Delhi: Motilal Banarsidass.

Duggan, L. (2003) *The Twilight of Equality? Neoliberalism, Cultural Politics, and the Attack on Democracy*. Boston: Beacon Press.

Dutta, A. (2013) 'Legible Identities and Legitimate Citizens: The Globalization of Transgender and Subjects of HIV-AIDS Prevention in Eastern India'. In *International Feminist Journal of Politics* 15:4.

Fernandez, B. (2002) *Humjinsi: A Resource Book on Lesbian, Gay and Bisexual Rights in India*. Mumbai: Combat Law Publications.

Fink, B. (2004) 'Reading "The Instance of the Letter in the Unconscious"' and 'Reading "The Subversion of the Subject"'. In *Lacan to the Letter: Reading Ecrits Closely*. Minneapolis: University of Minnesota Press.

Foucault, M. (1977) *Discipline and Punish: The Birth of the Prison* (Trans. Alan Sheridan). London: Penguin.

Foucault, M. (1978) *The History of Sexuality: An Introduction Volume I* (Trans. Robert Hurley). New York: Pantheon Books.

Foucault, M. (1980) 'Truth and Power'. In *Power/Knowledge: Selected Interviews and Other Writings 1972–1977* (Ed. Colin Gordon). New York: Pantheon Books.

Foucault, M. (2003) *Abnormal: Lectures at the College de France 1974–1975* (Trans. Graham Burchell; Ed: Arnold Davidson). New York: Picador.

Freccero, C. (2007) 'Queer Spectrality: Haunting the Past'. In *A Companion to Lesbian, Gay, Bisexual, Transgender and Queer Studies* (Eds. George E. Haggerty & Molly McGarry). Chichester: Blackwell.

Freud, S. (1905) *Three Essays on Sexuality*. London: Hogarth Press.

Freud, S. (1917/2006) 'Mourning and Melancholia'. In *The Penguin Freud Reader* (Ed. Adam Phillips). London: Penguin.

Gandhi, N. & Shah, N. (1992). *The issues at stake: Theory and practice in the contemporary women's movement in India*. New Delhi: Kali for Women.

Ghai, A. (2002) 'Disabled women: An excluded agenda of Indian feminism'. In *Hypatia* 17:3.

Ghai, A. (2005) 'Inclusive education: A myth or reality'. In *School, society, nation: Popular essays in education* (Eds. Rajni Kumar, Anil Sethi, & Shalini Sikka). New Delhi: Orient Longman.

Graham, L. & Slee, R. (2006) 'Inclusion?'. Paper presented in *Disability Studies in Education Special Interest Group, American Educational Research Association (AERA) 2006 Annual Conference*, 6–11 April 2006, San Francisco.

Gross, A. (2017) 'Post/Colonial Queer Globalization and International Human Rights: Images of LGBT Rights'. In *New Intimacies, Old Desires: Law, Culture and Queer Politics in Neoliberal Times* (Eds. Oishik Sircar & Dipika Jain). New Delhi: Zubaan.

Guha, R. (1982). 'On Some Aspects of the Historiography of Colonial India'. In *Subaltern Studies I: Writings on South Asian History and Society* (Ed. Ranajit Guha). New Delhi: Oxford University Press.

Guha, R. (1983) 'The Prose of Counter Insurgency'. In *Subaltern Studies II: Writings on South Asian History and Society* (Ed. Ranajit Guha). New Delhi: Oxford University Press.

Guha, R. (1989) 'Dominance Without Hegemony And Its Historiography'. In *Subaltern Studies VI: Writings on South Asian History and Society* (Ed. Ranajit Guha). New Delhi: Oxford University Press.

Guru, G. (1995) 'Dalit Women Talk Differently'. In *Economic and Political Weekly*, October.

Halberstam, J. (1998/2012) *Female Masculinity*. New Delhi: Zubaan.

Haritaworn, J. (2017) 'Beyond "Hate": Queer Metonymies of Crime, Pathology and Anti-/Violence'. In *New Intimacies, Old Desires: Law, Culture and Queer Politics in Neoliberal Times* (Eds. Oishik Sircar & Dipika Jain). New Delhi: Zubaan.

Haritaworn, J., Kuntsman, A., & Posocco, S. (2013) 'Murderous Inclusions'. In *International Feminist Journal of Politics* 15:4.

Jagose, A. (1996) *Queer Theory: An Introduction*. New York: New York University Press.

John, M.E. (2008) *Women's Studies in India: A Reader*. New Delhi: Penguin.

John, M.E. & Nair, J. (1998) 'Introduction'. In *The Question of Silence? The Sexual Economies of Modern India* (Eds. Mary John & Janaki Nair). New Delhi: Kali for Women.

John, M.E. & Niranjana, T. (2000) 'Introduction – The controversy over "Fire": a select dossier (Part I)'. In *Inter-Asia Cultural Studies* 1:2.

Judge, M. (2018) *Blackwashing Homophobia: Violence and the Politics of Sexuality, Gender and Race*. London: Routledge.

Kapur, R. (2009). 'Out of the Colonial Closet, but Still Thinking inside the Box: Regulating Perversion and the Role of Tolerance in Deradicalising the Rights Claims of Sexual Subalterns'. In *National University of Juridical Sciences Law Review*: 2.

Katyal, A. (2016) *The Doubleness of Sexuality: Idioms of Same-Sex Desire in Modern India*. New Delhi: New Text.

Kavi, A. (2007) 'Kothi versus Other MSM: Identity versus Behavior in the Chicken and Egg Paradox'. In *The Phobic and the Erotic: The Politics of Sexualities in Contemporary India* (Eds. Brinda Bose & Shubhabrata Bhattacharyya). Calcutta: Seagull.

khanna, a. (2007) 'Us "Sexuality Types": A Critical Engagement with the Postcoloniality of Sexuality'. In *The Phobic and the Erotic: The Politics of Sexualities in Contemporary India* (Eds. Brinda Bose & Shubhabrata Bhattacharyya). Calcutta: Seagull.

khanna, a. (2016) *Sexualness*. New Delhi: New Text.

Kumar, R. (1997). *The History of Doing: An Illustrated Account of Movements for Women's Rights and Feminism in India 1800–1990*. New Delhi: Zubaan.

LABIA (2013) *Breaking the Binary: Understanding Concerns and Realities of Queer Persons Assigned Gender Female at Birth across a Spectrum of Lived Gender Realities*. Mumbai: *LABIA*.

Lacan, J. (1949/2006) 'The Mirror Stage as Formative of the *I* Function as Revealed in Psychoanalytic Experience'. In *Ecrits: The First Complete Edition in English* (Trans. Bruce Fink). New York: W.W. Norton.

Lacan, J. (1957/2006) 'The Instance of the Letter in the Unconscious, or Reason Since Freud'. In *Ecrits: The First Complete Edition in English* (Trans. Bruce Fink). New York: W.W. Norton.

Lacan, J. (1958/2006) 'The Signification of the Phallus'. In *Ecrits: The First Complete Edition in English* (Trans. Bruce Fink). New York: W.W. Norton.

Lacan, J. (1960/2006) 'The Subversion of the Subject and the Dialectic of Desire in the Freudian Unconscious'. In *Ecrits: The First Complete Edition in English* (Trans. Bruce Fink). New York: W.W. Norton.

Lacan, J. (1964/2006) 'On Freud's "Trieb" and the Psychoanalyst's Desire'. In *Ecrits: The First Complete Edition in English* (Trans. Bruce Fink). New York: W.W. Norton.

Lacan, J. (1966/2006) 'Seminar on "The Purloined Letter"'. In *Ecrits: The First Complete Edition in English* (Trans. Bruce Fink). New York: W.W. Norton.

Lacquer, T. (1990) *Making Sex: Body and Gender from the Greeks to Freud*. Cambridge, MA: Harvard University Press.

Lear, J. (1998) 'Knowingness and Abandonment: An Oedipus for Our Time'. In *Open Minded: Working Out the Logic of the Soul*. Massachusetts: Harvard University Press.

Menon, N. (2007) 'Introduction' and 'Outing Heteronormativity: Nation, Citizen, Feminist Disruptions'. In *Sexualities* (Ed. Nivedita Menon). New Delhi: Kali for Women.

Mills, C. (2014) *Decolonizing Global Mental Health: The Psychiatrization of the Majority World*. London: Routledge.

Mitchell, J. (1974) *Psychoanalysis and Feminism*. New York: Pantheon.

Narrain, A. (2007a) 'No Shortcuts to Queer Utopia: Sodomy, Law, and Social Change'. In *The Phobic and the Erotic: The Politics of Sexualities in Contemporary India* (Eds. Brinda Bose & Shubhabrata Bhattacharyya). Calcutta: Seagull.

Narrain, A. (2007b) 'Queer Struggles Around The Law: The Contemporary Context'. In *Sexualities* (Ed. Nivedita Menon). New Delhi: Kali for Women.

Narrain, A. & Bhan, G. (2005) 'Introduction'. In *Because I Have a Voice: Queer Politics in India*. New Delhi: Yoda Press.

Narrain, A. & Gupta, A. (2011) 'Introduction'. In *Law Like Love: Queer Perspectives on Law*. New Delhi: Yoda Press.

Nilsen, A. & Roy, S. (2015) 'Introduction: Reconceptualizing Subaltern Politics in Contemporary India'. In *New Subaltern Studies: Reconceptualizing Hegemony and Resistance in Contemporary India* (Eds. Alf Gunvald Nilsen & Srila Roy). New Delhi: Oxford University Press.

Oliviera, J.M., Costa, C.G., & Carniero, N.S. (2014) 'Troubling Humanity: Towards a Queer Feminist Critical Psychology'. In *Annual Review of Critical Psychology* 11.

Pandit, M. (2013) 'Gendered Subaltern Sexuality and the State'. In *Economic and Political Weekly* Vol. XLVIII, No. 32.

Parker, I. (2011) 'Introduction' and 'Framing Analysis'. In *Lacanian Psychoanalysis: Revolutions in Subjectivity*. London: Routledge.

Pateman, C. (1988) *Sexual Contract*. Cambridge: Polity Press.

Pateman, C. (1989) *The Disorder of Women*. California: Stanford University Press.

Penney, J. (2014) 'The Universal Alternative'. In *After Queer Theory: The Limits of Sexual Politics*. London: Pluto Press.

People's Union for Civil Liberties, Karnataka (PUCL-K) (2001) *Human Rights Violations against Sexual Minorities in India: A Case Study of Bangalore*. Retrieved from www.pucl.org/Topics/Gender/2003/sexual-minorities.pdf.

Prakash, G. (1994) 'Subaltern Studies as Postcolonial Criticism'. In *American Historical Review* 99:5.

Puar, J. (1998) 'Transnational Sexualities: South Asian (trans)nation(alism)s and queer diasporas'. In *Q&A: Queer in Asian America* (Eds. David L. Eng & Alice Y. Hom). Philadelphia: Temple University Press.

Puar, J. (2007) *Terrorist Assemblages: Homonationalism in Queer Times*. Durham: Duke University Press.

Puar, J. (2017) 'Homonationalism as Assemblage: Viral Travels, Affective Sexualities'. In *New Intimacies, Old Desires: Law, Culture and Queer Politics in Neoliberal Times* (Eds. Oishik Sircar & Dipika Jain). New Delhi: Zubaan.

Ranciere, J. (1992) 'Politics, Identification, and Subjectivization'. In *October*, Vol. 61, The Identity in Question.

Rege, S. (1998) 'Dalit Women Talk Differently: A Critique of "Difference" and Towards a Dalit Feminist Standpoint Position'. In *Economic and Political Weekly*, October.

Rege, S. (2006) 'Introduction' and 'Debating the Consumption of Dalit "Autobiographies": The Significance of Dalit "Testimonios"'. In *Writing Caste Writing Gender*. New Delhi: Zubaan.
Roy, S. (2015) 'Affective Politics and the Sexual Subaltern: Lesbian Activism in Eastern India'. In *New Subaltern Studies: Reconceptualizing Hegemony and Resistance in Contemporary India* (Eds. Alf Gunvald Nilsen & Srila Roy). New Delhi: Oxford University Press.
Rubin, G. (2011) *Deviations: A Gayle Rubin Reader*. Durham: Duke University Press.
Samaddar, R. (2010) *Emergence of the Political Subject*. New Delhi: Sage.
Santiago, S. (2002) 'The Wily Homosexual (First-and Necessarily Hasty-Notes)'. In *Queer Globalizations: Citizenship and the Afterlife of Colonialism* (Eds. Arnaldo Cruz-Maave & Martin F. Manalansan IV). New York: New York University Press.
Sappho for Equality (2010) *Of Horizons and Beyond: Glimpses of Lesbians, Bisexual Women and Transpersons' Lives*. Kolkata: *Sappho for Equality*.
Sappho for Equality (2011) *Vio-Map: Documenting and Mapping Violence and Rights Violation Taking Place in Lives of Sexually Marginalized Women and Transmen to Chart Out Effective Advocacy Strategies*. Kolkata: *Sappho for Equality*.
Sappho for Equality (Producer), Majumder, D. (Director) (2013) *Ebong Bewarish (. . . And the Unclaimed)*. India: *Sappho for Equality*.
Scott, J. (1992) 'Experience'. In *Feminists Theorize the Political* (Eds. Judith Butler & Joan Scott). London: Routledge.
Sedgwick, E. (1990) 'Introduction: Axiomatic'. In *Epistemology of the Closet*. Berkeley: University of California Press.
Sen, R. (2016) 'Women with Disabilities: Cartographic Encounters with Legal Interstices'. In *Indian Anthropologist: Everyday State and Politics* 46:2.
Shah, C. (2005) 'The Roads that E/Merged: Feminist Activism and Queer Understanding'. In *Because I Have a Voice: Queer Politics in India*. New Delhi: Yoda Press.
Siddiqui, S. (2016) *Religion and Psychoanalysis in India: Critical Clinical Practice*. London: Routledge.
Sircar, O. & Jain, D. (2017) 'Introduction: Of Powerful Feelings and Facile Gestures'. In *New Intimacies, Old Desires: Law, Culture and Queer Politics in Neoliberal Times*. New Delhi: Zubaan.
Spivak, G.C. (1976/2002) 'Translator's Preface'. In *Of Grammatology* (Trans. Gayatri Spivak). Delhi: Motilal Banarsidass.
Spivak, G.C. (1985) 'Subaltern Studies: Deconstructing Historiography'. In *Subaltern Studies IV: Writings on South Asian History and Society* (Ed. Ranajit Guha). New Delhi: Oxford University Press.
Spivak, G.C. (1987) 'A Literary Representation of the Subaltern: Mahasweta Devi's "Stanadayini"'. In *Subaltern Studies V: Writings on South Asian History and Society* (Ed. Ranajit Guha). New Delhi: Oxford University Press.
Spivak, G.C. (1987/2014) '"Breast-giver": For Author, Teacher, Subaltern, Historian . . .'. In Mahasweta Devi, *Breast Stories* (Trans. Gayatri Chakravorty Spivak). Kolkata: Seagull.

Spivak, G.C. (1988) 'Can the Subaltern Speak?'. In *Marxism and the Interpretation of Culture* (Eds. C. Nelson & L. Grossberg). Basingstoke: Macmillan Education.

Spivak, G.C. (1993/2012) 'Woman in Difference'. In *Outside in the Teaching Machine*. New York: Routledge.

Spivak, G.C. (2004) 'The Trajectory of the Subaltern in My Work'. *Voices*. Talk retrieved from www.youtube.com/watch?v=2ZHH4ALRFHw.

Spivak, G.C. (2005) 'Scattered Speculations on the subaltern and the popular'. In *Postcolonial Studies* 8:4.

Stephens, J. (1989) 'Feminist fictions: A critique of the category "non western woman" in feminist writings on India'. In *Subaltern Studies VI: Writings on South Asian History and Society* (Ed. Ranajit Guha). New Delhi: Oxford University Press.

Sunder Rajan, R. (2003) 'Representing Sati: Continuities and Discontinuities'. In *Real and Imagined Women: Gender, culture and postcolonialism*. London: Routledge.

Sutanuka, Shraddha, & Poushali (2014) 'Self Determination of Gender: The Trans Experience'. In *Swakanthey – in our own voice*, 11: 2. Kolkata: *Sappho for Equality*.

Thadani, G. (1996) *Sakhiyani: Lesbian Desire in Ancient and Modern India*. London: Cassell.

Tosh, J. (2015) *Perverse Psychology: The pathologization of sexual violence and transgenderism*. London: Routledge.

Upadhya, C. (1998) 'Set this house on Fire'. In *Economic and Political Weekly*, December.

Upadhyay, N. & Ravecca, P. (2017) 'Queer, Beyond Queer?'. In *New Intimacies, Old Desires: Law, Culture and Queer Politics in Neoliberal Times* (Eds. Oishik Sircar & Dipika Jain). New Delhi: Zubaan.

Vanita, R. & Kidwai, S. (2008) *Same-Sex Love in India: A Literary History*. New Delhi: Penguin.

Ziering, A. & Kofman, G. (Producers), Ziering, A. & Dick, K. (Directors) (2002) *Derrida*. USA: Zeitgeist Films.

Zubaan (2006) *Poster Women: A Visual History of the Women's Movement in India*. New Delhi: Zubaan.

Zupancic, A. (2016) 'Biopolitics, Sexuality and the Unconscious'. In *Paragraph* 39:1.

INDEX

Page numbers in *italics* show an illustration, n indicates an endnote

ABVA (*AIDS Bhedbhav Virodhi Andolan*) 13–14, 20
Arendt, H. 88
Arnold, D. 109

Bacchetta, P. 29
Bandyopadhyay, S. 28
Bhaduri, B. 79, 106
Bhan, G. 13–14, 21, 30, 31
Bhattacharyya, S. 30
bisexual women 19–20, 26–27
Bose, B. 30
Brown, W. 45
Butler, J. 50, 52, 58, 124–125, 127

Caleri (*Campaign for Lesbian Rights*) 14, 16, 17, 27
Chakrabarty, D. 100
Chiesa, L. 54, 57, 73–74
Chow, R. 70–71
colonialism and subaltern subordination 98–99

critical psychology 6
Cuellar, D. 55, 85

Dave, N. 14, 15–16, 26
Derrida, J. 47, 88–89, 119

Ebong Bewarish (*. . . And the Unclaimed*) 4, 69, 85–86

Faroqui, V. 16
feminism and queer politics 61–62, 65n1
Fink, B. 56
Fire (Mehta), reactions to 14, 15, 18, 28
Forum against Oppression of Women (*FAOW*) 14
Foucault, M. 50, 52
Freud, S. 124–125, 126

Graham, L. 47, 48–49
Guha, R. 95–99, 100, 101
Gupta, A. 110, 111

Index

Haritaworn, J. 46
heteronormativity, rejection and violence 75–78
hijra 19, 20, 21, 30, 40
homonationalism 3
homosexuality, queer taxonomy 30–33
human rights and queerness: inclusion, process and costs 45–50; marginalized experience 31, 42; naturalizing of experience 42–43

identity politics: cultural specificity 25–26; internet and Western influences 27–28; lesbian subjectivity 26–28; queerness 2–3; queer taxonomy and radical potential 30–33
Immoral Traffic Prevention Act (ITPA) 40
Indian Association of Women's Studies (IAWS) 18

Jagori 17
Jagose, A. 32

Kapur, R. 109, 110–111
khanna, a. 40
kothis 19, 21, 30

LABIA 23, 24; see also Stree Sangam
Lacan, J.: conscious subject and ego ideal 52–55; desire and metonymic function 72–74, 78; language, the *other* and process of desire 56–59, 72–73, 75; L schema, intersubjectivity *59*, 59–60; metonymy and displacement 54–55, 71–72; the other (mirror stage) 55
lesbian activism: gay men's patriarchy 19–20; group formations 17–18, 23–24; transnational funding divide 22–23; women's movements, mixed response 14–19

lesbianism: identity and subjectivity 26–28; lesbian suicides, representation of 77, 81
LesBit 24–25

Menon, N. 29, 31
Men who have Sex with Men (MSM) 21, 30, 40
Mondal, Swapna and Sucheta: class, caste and community 80–81; death investigation, community hostility 86–87; death as lesbian suicide 82; gender identity, manipulation of 78–79; heteronormativity, rejection and violence 75–78; political representation 83–84, 120–121; representation through narrative 69–70; *Sappho for Equality* representation 4, 77, 78–79, 82–83, 85–86; as sexual subaltern subjects 113, 121–122, 126–127; Sucheta's husband suicide attempt 79; suicide letter, transfer of signification 71–73, 75; Swapna's suicide letter 9, 35, 67, 91, 117, 118n1
Mothers of Manipur 63
movements, political/social 11–13

Narrain, A. 13–14, 21, 30, 31, 110, 111
Naz Foundation and Lawyers Collective 20
Nilsen, A. 111
No Going Back 20

OLAVA (*Organized Lesbian Alliance for Visibility and Action*) 17

Penney, J. 93
pinkwashing 2–3
Prakash, G. 95, 103
PRISM 20
psychoanalysis and political theory 6–7
Puar, J. 28

Index

queerness: human rights and inclusion 31, 41–43, 45–50; identity politics 2–3, 25–28, 30–33; interpretation and articulation 1–2, 5–6, 37–38, 43–45

queer political subject: 'citizen-militant', power/resistance dialectic 38–40; inclusion, process and costs 45–50, 88–89; legitimacy of experience and unification 43–45, 50–51, 83–84; political and psychoanalytic resistance 59–60, 59–64; relations of power 51, 83; rights discourse, citizenship and identity 40–43; subjectivity, theories applied 52–59

queer politics, India: emergence history 13–14; gender differences 19–20; neoliberalism and globalization impacts 23–25, 93–94, 120; queer taxonomy, cultural and political change 29–33, 119–121; Section 377, activism against 20–21; sexuality and nationalism 28–29; transnational funding 21–23; women's movements, mixed response 14–19

representation: heteronormative society, positions within 75–79, 108; objectivity and interpretation 70–71; process of proxy and reassertion 82–84, 103–106, 127; by proxy 71; psychoanalytical framework 85–86; questioning authorization 86–89; Swapna's letter, transfer of signification 71–73, 75

Rights of Transgender Persons Bill 2014 3, 49

Roy, S. 110–111

Sakhi 14, 26

Samaddar, R. 38–39, 40–41, 63

Sangini 17

Sappho for Equality: changing focus 23–24; formation 17; lesbian suicide 77, 81; member representation questioned 87–88, 89; Mondal deaths, factual report 4; Mondal deaths investigation, community hostility 86–87; representation of Swapna and Sucheta Mondal 69–70, 77, 78–79, 80, 82–83; sexuality, community reactions 80

Scott, J. 42–43, 44

Section 377, Indian Penal Code 20–21, 40, 62

sexuality: melancholia and gender 124–126, 127; personal choice 41–42; queerness defined 2, 41

sexual subaltern subject: concepts and criticisms 109–111, 115n2; queer politics 113–114, 127; research approaches evaluated 122–124, 127–128

Shah, C. 15, 19

Slee, R. 47, 49

Spivak, G.: articulation through death 79, 106; representation by proxy and reconstruction 71, 103–106, 127; subalterns, non-identity and mobility 107–108; subaltern studies critique 101–103; subaltern women as focus 101–102, 104

Stree Sangam 14, 17, 27; *see also* LABIA

Subaltern Studies Collective: Guha's contribution 95–99, 100, 101; Spivak's critique 103; study origins 94–95; theory revisions 107, 108

subaltern subject: contemporary concepts and differentiations 108–109, 110–113; elitist bias to political historiography 95–97; emergence history 94–95; figure without consciousness 97–98; gendered focus 101–102, 104–106; non-identity and social mobility 107–108; redefining own and

national history 99–101; representation by proxy and reconstruction 104–106; representation failure, study critique 102–103; sexual subaltern and queer politics 113–114; sexual subaltern, concepts and criticisms 109–111, 115n2; sexual subaltern, research considerations 122–124; subordination under colonialism 98–99
subjectivation 50–51
subjectivity, theories of: Foucault's subjectivation 52; Lacan's conscious and subconscious subject 52–59; Lacan's L schema 59, 59–60

Thackeray, B. 28
Transgender Persons (Protection of Rights) Bill 2016 3
transgender subjects 3
transnational funding 21–23

Voices against 377 20

women's movements, India: gender and sexuality 13–14; mapping critiques 12–13; National Conferences 19; queer activism, convergence and resistance 14–19; transnational influences 15–16, 22–23